If Her *Purse* Could Talk

A transparent journey into the lives
of women who courageously reveal the contents of their heart

Compiled By
DeYonne Parker

Gem Makers
Publishing

Dedication

This book is dedicated to all the women whose
purses got too heavy for them to carry.
May the truth of our stories help
lighten your load.

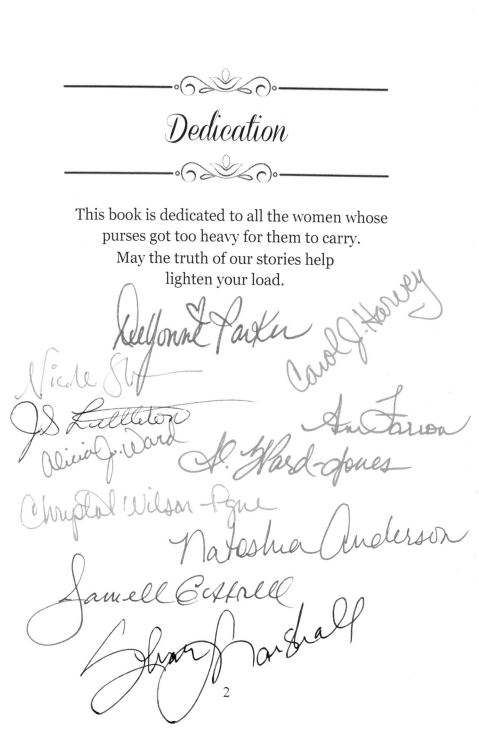

Table of Contents

My Purse

Speaks Louder Than Words

Chapter 1

Our Purses Tell Stories

How often do you change your purse? You know what I mean, rotate in a new style or vibrant color to match the latest fashion you might be rocking that week or maybe even that month. Or maybe you're a daring diva that likes to throw caution to the wind and rock an evening purse that's adorned with bold spikes, sparkles or spots that have your onlooker's eyes bulging. So, are you a daily, weekly or monthly purse changer?

Well, I hate to admit it, but I don't change my purse that often. In fact, it might be several months before I rotate my purse of choice. And if we're *really* being honest, because I travel quite often, I'm rocking a very spacious black book bag that's playing host to my purse right now. I know some of you Fashionistas might be cringing right now at the very thought, but that's my current reality!

I don't always have time to change my purse. Sure, I have a trusty few that can go with any outfit that I wear and a few others that I can put into rotation that are fun and fashionable. But, I pretty much latch on to a strong, sturdy, stylish purse and put it to work!

When I do change my purse I sometimes leave behind a few items that don't need to carry over to the new one. You know...stuff like receipts, trinkets, candy, kid's toys, church programs and other worn out things that need not make an appearance in the chosen purse for that season.

So, standing in my closet and looking at my purses, I decided it was time to commit to the dreaded task...cleaning out all my purses, including the one that I was currently toting. As I began to pull stuff out of the various handbags and examine them to see if there was anything worth salvaging, I began to see where I'd been during the different seasons in my life. From the receipts, airline tickets, make-up and various sticky notes, I could tell where I'd spent my time, money and my energy.

Something struck me in that moment. You may think what you run across in the bottom of a purse is just left behind junk (and sometimes it is) but, when you look a little closer you'll be able to see the depth of a woman - who she is and what she cares about. Just like her, on the outside of a purse you may see flash, fringe and fashion, but on the inside you may find things that represent passion, pain and purpose.

A simple receipt may look like a list of grocery items purchased, but upon further investigation, the items on the list may have been purchased to care for someone else in their time of need. A bag of treats or snacks may be in tote as a planned surprise for a school-age child or to calm a fussy toddler on a long drive. A pack of tissues may have landed amongst the contents of her purse to dry her eyes as she perseveres through some of the toughest challenges in her life or to nurse a cold she received from graciously loving on others in her family circle.

The handwritten notes that found their way to the bottom of her purse may be messages the Lord deposited in her spirit that will later be shared with the world in the form of a book. Or they may be things she needs to remember to do for others she thoughtfully cares for.

The various types of make-up products in her make-up bag or scattered throughout may be used to help her put on the face the world expects her to present every day or to hide the dark circles under her eyes from multiple sleepless nights. And just like the heart of a woman, other people's things may have made their way into her purse because they no longer wanted to carry them and assumed she had space for their things too.

As I began putting away the purses now spread out before me, I noticed some were tattered and torn around the straps and some had gaping holes in the bottom of the lining. I realized this must have been caused from the weight of all the things I was struggling to carry around during that season. I stopped and began to thank God for the revelation that He was giving me through my purses. I thanked Him for carrying me through these seasons of my life and filling the gaping holes that threatened to tear me down.

Just as those purses had carried around the weight of the contents, I was grateful to my Savior for carrying the weight that I had inside of me. As I began to replace the acceptable items back into my current purse of the season, I wondered about the journey it would take with me and prayed that it had the strength to go the distance!

Courageously Opening Our Purses

If you're a woman who carries a purse, I'm sure you're all too familiar with how it feels when someone attempts to open your purse and rummage through the contents WITHOUT your permission. Not only does the invasive intruder get a stern look, but they might receive a slap on the hand or even the back of the head (I'm just saying!).

A woman's purse is sacred. We carry some of everything in them, from personal items to priceless possessions. As a result, we guard and protect them from anyone or anything that might pose a threat to it or the contents inside.

The chapters in this book are much like a woman's purse, personal and private. I, along with 11 other courageous women, invite you to open our "purses" and take a peek inside. You'll find that our stories are transparent, transformational and provides an honest answer to the question, "If your purse could talk, what would it say?"

As you read each chapter, my desire is that you'll see glimpses of yourself in at least one or maybe all of our stories. By the time you have finished reading our stories, I hope you will feel inspired and courageous enough to look a little deeper into the contents of your "purse" and find your own story.

Give yourself permission to shine a light on what you've been carrying and challenge yourself to truthfully answer the question, *"If your purse could talk, what would it say?"*

I encourage you to grab a pen, a journal and maybe a group of friends to read along with you. It's about to get deep!

Welcome to the inside of our purses. Enjoy the journey.

~ DeYonne Parker ~

Chapter 2

1 Am Not My Purse

By Ann Farrow

Why aren't I colorful like other purses? Why don't I have sparkles, glitter or designer labels on me like other purses? I get that my main purpose is to be functional and practical. I get that I was bought to serve a purpose, not to be a fashion accessory. I'm okay with that, but sometimes I wonder...is there more to me than this?

If my purse could talk, I'd imagine that is what it might say in those quiet moments when it's alone on my bed; it's work for the day complete. I was never that woman who had to have a lot of purses in a myriad of shapes, sizes and colors. At any given point in my adult life, one thing you could count on was that no matter the occasion, on my shoulder would be the same type of purse – a functional, black leather purse. Over the years it has grown in size – motherhood and adulting will do that – but it was consistently black, leather, one strap just long enough and wide enough to comfortably sit on my shoulder, silver zipper and clasps. It would have one main area with 1-3 small pockets on the inside for keys

12

and other items that easily get lost in the main section.

It's not that I deeply ponder over different bags and then choose a black purse as my main purse (actually, my *only* purse for most of my adult life) instead of other colors or unique styles; it's just what I've always bought. It makes sense to me – black goes with everything, right? With a black purse, there's no figuring out if the purse is the right shade that matches my shoes, belt or dress. I don't have to transfer important items from one purse to another when I want to switch up. Basically, having only one purse and that one purse being black is just *easier*.

I've accepted that I'm just not the kind of woman who is into purses, who gets giddy from seeing *that purse* in the department store. Whose eyes glaze over and I momentarily lose the ability to speak in coherent sentences when I see the newest Michael Kors bag for sale. Will I acknowledge that it's nice? Of course, who wouldn't? But then I will adjust the strap of my black purse and move on. Yep, I'm pretty sure the phrase, "I gotta have that purse!" has never, ever left my mouth (or shoes for that matter, but that's another story)!

But...what if always buying one black, leather, functional purse speaks to a deeper, underlying reason other than it's just easier? What if the choice of that practical black purse connects to a deep-seated belief that there's no flashiness, no pizazz, no sparkle *in me?*

Even though I wasn't that girly girl growing up, it seemed logical that as I aged, established myself and earned more money, having different purses that I liked would be normal for me. Over the years I've gone to functions and events that easily justified the purchase of a new outfit and accessories, including a pretty matching purse. But I didn't buy it.

Why?

When I got married in 1996, I was already a mother. Corey, my firstborn, was and continues to be a gift from God. Yet, that time of my life was the culmination of a season of failure, lack, shame, and regret. I wasn't supposed to be that girl who had a child out of wedlock. I was the smart one, the one who was supposed to get a college degree and go far in life. I earned a bachelor of science degree in physics, was awarded a six-figure fellowship that covered all of my graduate school expenses, and was accepted into a doctoral program in high-energy physics.

I was also a Christian. I gave my life to Christ the spring semester of my freshman year in college. Within a month I was baptized in the Holy Spirit and began studying the Bible with a staff member at my college who had started a Bible study on campus. I was reading Hebrew-Greek and Amplified translations as an 18 year-old, looking up the meanings of Bible phrases in my concordance, spending my free time praying or talking about God to my Christian friends. While others were struggling with how to live a godly life or dealing with problem relationships, I was focused on reading God's Word and doing the right things. It all seemed so simple – if the Bible says do it, do it. If it says don't do it, well, don't do it. I couldn't understand why so many Christians were struggling with being obedient to the Word.

Until my senior year.

That's when things began to get confusing for me. I'd been watching other Christians "play Christian" for three years. They were singing in the on-campus Baptist choir, attending Sunday service, praying in our intercessory prayer meetings by day and having sex, drinking, gossiping and starting rumors about others by night. *And nothing bad happened to them.* Weren't they supposed to be punished for sinning like that?

When I read the Old Testament of the Bible, over and over I saw stories of God's people pretty much receiving what they deserved as a result of their behavior. When they obeyed God, they were rewarded with His protection, provision, and success (think Joshua and the wall of Jericho, King David's successes, God rewarding Solomon with wisdom, wealth and fame, God defeating three armies for King Jehoshaphat of Judah). When they disobeyed, they were punished with disease, death and failure (think the older generation of Israelites who died in the wilderness because of disobedience, the plagues that killed thousands while in the wilderness, the famines during the times of the prophets Elijah and Elisha, the children of Israel being driven away from the Promised Land in bondage because of their disobedience). To me it looked like other Christians my age were behaving just like students who weren't saved. To top it all off, the other Christians seemed happy. They weren't walking around in shame or guilt. They weren't hiding from others, feeling unworthy.

In contrast, I had been diligently obeying God and His Word – but was unhappy. I was lonely, unfulfilled, uncomfortable with myself, and uncertain of my purpose. I was handling my business in the classroom, involved in extra-curricular activities, but my life was unexciting and purposeless. *It wasn't fair.*

I decided that if the other Christians could have their cake and eat it too, then so could I.

The first time I had sex was in a dorm room with a guy who I had met while at a summer research program. It was – an empty experience. I was attracted to him, but I didn't really want to have sex with him. It was what he wanted and expected; he could care less that I was a virgin and I didn't care enough that I was a child of God and worth more than that. So in a matter of moments (literally, it was not what you read about in romance novels!) I traded everything I knew about God and thought I knew about me – for what? An unfulfilling, insignificant experience.

That one decision didn't give me one ounce of fulfillment or pleasure, but it did give me a boatload of shame and guilt.

Fast forward to my time in graduate school. I was in a relationship with the man I would eventually marry who is the father of my three children. Our relationship was sexual and we were living together (to save money of course). I knew that this kind of relationship was totally against God's will but I chose to do it anyway and I walked in guilt and shame all the time because of that choice. Eventually I got pregnant and I dropped out of grad school. Out of school and jobless, my older sister drove to Michigan, packed me up, and took me and my six-month old son to my parents' house – the home I grew up in.

Total, complete, full-blown failure.

Even after I got married a year after Corey was born, the shame and regret stuck to me like glue. In my mind I was a complete disappointment to God, my family and myself. I prayed for forgiveness, promised to be the best Christian, wife and mother that I could be, yet I still hated myself for the choices I'd made. For choosing my own desires over God. For being a total hypocrite, for "playing Christian".

That season, from my time in grad school to the early years of my marriage, was my personal desert. There was a barrenness in my life where there was little joy, power, or success. The sin and the shame cast a continual shadow over me, eliciting this constant thought that *I deserve every bad thing that happens and I don't deserve good things to happen to me at all.* So I put my head down and worked to be a good mother and a godly wife. I no longer dreamed to be the best me because I no longer deserved to have hopes and dreams.

It showed in how I treated myself. I didn't treat myself poorly. I just never thought to treat myself special. No manicures, no shopping for pretty things that made me feel special. I only bought what I needed. A black leather purse was all that I needed.

You see, I wasn't walking around telling everybody about my shame and guilt. On the outside, I was smiling, helpful, loving, and nice to everyone. I was good at wearing the "I'm good" mask.

However, that simple black leather purse represented the chronic shame I kept hidden. It represented the consistent thought I had about myself behind the smile; the thought that I couldn't move past – no, that I didn't *deserve* to move past – my mistakes. And I didn't even realize it.

My son is now 22 years old; my daughters are 20 and 16. I've experienced loss – my father, my marriage, and my home. I went back to graduate school; I got closer to my Ph.D. this time but still didn't finish. Loss and failure haven't disappeared from my life.

But I've also experienced and continue to experience wonderful things. I've grown in my walk with God. I am living in a space where I have a deeper understanding of God and how to experience His love and grace in my everyday life. My black-and-white, legalistic mindset that had me thinking that God treats us according to our behavior has disappeared. More than ever, I see God's grace, that unmerited favor, at work in my life and the lives of my children. I rest in the truth that it's always been about my relationship with God, not His rules. Learning to obey Him out of reverence and love instead of fear of punishment has allowed me to abide in a state of peace more often than not. My focus is no longer on being perfect, but on allowing His perfection to define me.

I still have my black leather purse. In sitting down to write this, I realize that there are areas in my life where I'm still only existing, not living. Even as my life is moving forward and God is transforming me, I haven't totally broken that habit of only getting what I need.

However, there are signs of change.

Every so often, I do something nice for myself. It's not consistent and it's not big things, but they make me smile. I'll buy jewelry to go with an outfit when I only intended to buy the dress. I'll add color to my hair to change it up sometimes. And I am slowly beginning to dream again – about fun things I'd like to do, about my future, about love.

My heart is finally beginning to accept what my head has known for a while – that I am more than my mistakes. That failure is an event in my life, not my identity. That I will continue to make mistakes because I'm human, but I can always go to God when I do because He's not.

And guess what? Now, I have two red purses and a second black purse that's fancier than my everyday black bag. They were gifts, but I actually carry them when I think they go better with my outfit. And I don't mind moving all my stuff from one purse to another!

I haven't gotten to the point where I am considering buying that bedazzled, blinged-out purse you would notice from a mile away (and to be honest, you probably shouldn't hold your breath on that one!) but I'm slowly progressing to the place where I consider buying nice things just because I like them. I'll probably always think about its practicality before buying a purse – I think it's just part of my nature. But the peeling back of the layers of shame has uncovered the real me who believes it's okay to want my purse to be more than just practical; it can also have some "wow" to it! Because there's a lot of "wow" in me! Who knows – maybe one day you'll see this gorgeous, colorful unique purse, and when you look up it will be on *my* shoulder. Now if *that* purse could talk, what would it say?

Purse Prayer:

Heavenly Father, I pray everyone who reads this chapter and has ever lived with regret or shame for past decisions will understand that there is nothing that You won't forgive. May they hear and accept that they are so much more than their worst mistake. I pray that they release all guilt and never, ever pick it back up again. Instead, let them receive Your forgiveness and grace and experience the transformation of Your love. I pray that the masks of mediocrity based on the past will be broken into a million pieces and that when they look in the mirror they see the reflection of the amazing, beautiful, powerful women they were called to be. I pray that every black purse purchased and worn is by choice, not by a limited belief in what one thinks they deserve. Let every person reading this chapter live, love and dream to fullest extent possible. In Jesus' name, Amen.

Ann Farrow

Ann Farrow is a born and bred suburbanite, hailing from Prince Georges County, MD. After high school, she attended Prairie View A&M University in Prairie View Texas, where she received her Bachelors of Science degree in physics.

Afterwards, she traveled to the Midwest to pursue her Ph.D. in high energy physics.

Realizing this was not quite her niche, she taught high school physics and started a family before deciding to re-enter graduate school, this time deciding to pursue a doctorate in sociology. She paused her doctoral pursuits in sociology at the ABD doctoral candidate status.

Ann believes in the power of the spoken and written word. As a research administrator at a liberal arts college, Ann helps to bring research, curriculum, and programmatic projects to life. In addition, she is the COO of Influencers Publishing, LLC, a digital publishing company that "nurtures the author within the influencer" and an aspiring voice-over artist and budding author.

One of her greatest joys is being the mother of three wonderful, uniquely gifted children. Ann is passionate about guiding others to live out their God-given purpose.

Chapter 3

My Secret Keeper
By FaLisa Ward-Jones

When my sister asked me to be a part of this project I was excited and admittedly also a little insecure. You see, as the youngest of three daughters, I have become quite good at listening, both when asked, and when I was caught ear hustling as they gathered around the family table. What I am not very good at is opening up to others about myself. I was blessed to come from a long line of women. From my beautiful and headstrong Grandmother and her 3 sisters, to my own mother and aunts, this family dynamic left me with many opportunities to listen and learn from the stories of their lives.

Grandma's Table

I loved every time we got together and all the women would sit around my grandparent's kitchen table, telling stories from that day or 20 years ago. I still remember the multi-colored flowers on the tablecloth and the doorway to the kitchen that had hanging wooden beads for us to walk through. They were my favorite things about their house.

As the Johnson and Hollingsworth women all sat around talking and laughing, I would sit on the corner of a nearby hutch that contained all my grandma's fine dishes because it was the only available spot in the kitchen; pretending that I wasn't listening.

As a kid, I don't know why I loved listening to them talk so much, but I was drawn by the laughter and whispered gossip that they tried to keep my grandpa from hearing and I didn't care how uncomfortable I was while sitting on the edge of that wooden hutch. Occasionally someone would catch me staring and say "Lisa get out of my mouth!" But sometimes, while they were deep in conversation, my grandma would notice me and appreciate my presence when she needed me to do something. She would say, "Lisa, go grab my pocket book". This is where she kept her secret stash of cigarettes that she didn't want my grandpa to know she had. Or my mother would send me to bring her purse to her and while bringing it, I would notice the full pack of gum popping out from the bottom, when she just told me she chewed her last piece in the car! This is when I began making the association of purses with secrets. Like a best friend, they offer a woman space to hide and protect things of value, without having to explain why.

So when my sister, DeYonne, (or Dee, as I affectionately call her) asked the question, "If your purse could talk, what would it say?" It forced me to provide an explanation of the space no one dared to enter into without asking. If my purse could talk, it would honestly expose things about me that I do not intend for most people to know. Or it would confirm their suspicions. It would probably scream from the weight of my past mixed in with the weight of my present and future and say "Lisa, for real... this is getting ridiculous. You have got to let go of something!"

Being raised as the youngest in a household of girls, I can remember being fearful of womanhood. The thought of what we referred to in my house as the "P" caused me more anxiety and stress than one can imagine. I was not the girl excited to become a woman. In fact, I was a 12 year old who turned my nose up at the thought of puberty the closer I got to it. The "P" symbolized the letting go of being care free and limitless, to being bound by that awful flow that would change my life forever! So I wasn't really too concerned about carrying a purse because at this point, I had nothing to conceal.

It was the summer of Batman – the legendary series that had been remade into a movie, starring Michael Keaton as Batman. If you were a kid of the 80's and remember that soundtrack- you know this movie was a big deal. My best friend Leah and I were so excited to go and see it! Leah was a cute, short girl, who was part Asian and black. She was always so confident and stylish. I was always so intrigued with how pretty she was. Next to her, I felt so tall and out of

26

place, but she was really fun to be around. She took dance lessons and I envied that because it was something I always wanted, but we couldn't afford. "Oh well!" I thought, I could still keep up with her. Leah and I choreographed our own dances to the movie soundtrack in her front yard. With our dance moves together and our synchronized steps, we were ready to go see this movie!

The day finally came – June 29th, 1989! I wasn't feeling that well when I woke up, but my excitement for the movie overshadowed my discomfort. It was the summer and my mother had to work, so she agreed to let me go with Leah and her Mom. We made our way to the movie, found our seats and settled in for what we'd been waiting for. We were so excited! Not long into the movie, my excitement turned into dread! My worst fear had come upon me! (to quote the scripture of Job in the worst way) I started my period right there in the movie theatre. I didn't freak out, but I remember feeling so embarrassed and alone because I wasn't with MY mama, but someone else's. As we made our way back to the house I was trying to keep my composure so no one would know. I laughed and talked about the movie with my friend, realizing I didn't know the details because I was no longer interested after my body disappointed me.

So now I had to break the news to my Mom over the phone, who was working two jobs at the time. I didn't want my sisters to know because I was afraid they would make fun of me. So I had to wait until the end of the night to be comforted by Mom. No one knew what this day really meant to me. My sisters dismissed it as a part of life and my mother talked me through it, but honestly I was hurt. You see, I was faced with having to let go of the first thing that really mattered to me...the thing that separated me and formed my identity to this point...my childhood.

After this experience, carrying a purse was no longer an option; it was a necessity. Not being thrilled about the changes, a cute purse wasn't of importance. Something functional and large enough to carry what I was trying so hard to hide was good enough. The days I would leave it at home only exposed the days I was trying to hide, so I realized then that my purse would be with me *forever*.

Functional but Fierce!

In the later stages of my life, my purse has taken on new meaning. It's still a concealer, but now one met with acceptance and I have a greater appreciation for this vessel. It has become much more than a hiding place. I would love to tell you that I carry the pretty, fancy, or expensive bags, but that would be a lie. I still go for function and style over name brand.

Anytime I shop for a purse (which is not very often) I wander the aisles looking through the different styles ranging from sensible and understated to the bold and fierce prints that

28

scream confidence. I feel like I'm a judge on one of the popular singing shows where each purse is doing its best performance to stand out. I hear them say how good they would look with my outfit and how I should try something new. But 95% of the time, I end up playing the role of Simon Cowell as I walk away saying – "sorry but it's a No for me".

I usually end up with a practical color that will go with any outfit. It's not an issue of value or even confidence, but a matter of what speaks to ME. Straying too far from that is always a challenge and I'll admit that in my 40's I'm still defining ME. My mother used to say "You know Lisa is not good with change – you can't change her direction in the middle of a stream". Well in those moments she was right, but as I think back over my life, I realize I've grown into a woman who learned how to conquer change with amazing resilience. Quite honestly, I didn't realize I possessed that character. But just like my modest purse, I may not be the boldest or flashiest in the group, but the strength that's concealed inside of me might go unnoticed to the naked eye. I may appear to be conservative on the outside, but my inner lining is FIERCE!

I was 22 when I decided to exchange my small home town, Omaha, NE, for the big city of Chicago, IL. It was all in the name of *Love* and his name was Quincy Jones. I never thought I would leave the only city I knew as home, but for him I did. I had been with him since I was 19 years old and my identity as a young woman was deeply woven into this relationship. He was the love of my young life. Even when things in our relationship didn't work out as planned, most thought I would pack up and move back home with my tail between my legs. I could have, but I decided to hold on to the life I was making here in the Windy City.

I found a great job and was excited about the possibilities of my career. But it came with a price. I fought many days of sadness after a failed long-term relationship. I was in a new place where not many I loved knew my name. I was figuring out how to navigate life as a young adult in what felt like a foreign land. So instead of moving back to the comforts of my stumping grounds, I decided to put on my big girl shoes and find the best studio apartment I could afford. One that had large picture windows in a high rise looking out to the picturesque Chicago Skyline. It was a teenage dream of mine to have an "apartment in the sky". I just never thought it would be in this large city.

To be honest, I actually didn't like living here at first. I was constantly overwhelmed with getting lost every week, or standing at the bus stop in the dark and cold rain waiting to go home from work. I had no idea how to ride the "L" train and found myself in some tough spots at the wrong time of day.

Unfortunately, there were a lot of dark days. Days I didn't

know how I was going to make it. Some days the depression consumed me to the point of calling in sick and not getting out of bed. I chose to keep a lot of this to myself because I didn't want to worry my mother and I was too proud to ask my ex for help. I can recall a time that my car had broken down, I had just enough money to pay my rent and get back and forth to work. Even buying groceries had even become a struggle.

My apartment in the sky was now starting to take on a different tone. The thought of packing up and leaving behind what I worked to establish was beginning to look like a more reasonable option at this point. But I was determined to make this work so, I worked two jobs for a while to make ends meet.

I was managing to get by and eventually a shift started to occur. I stopped getting lost and in fact, I began giving directions! I loved Chicago! I was dating again, meeting people out, dressing to impress and my purse, she was growing with me! She was becoming less about function and was now beginning to take on an identity of her own.

It was a rough road getting to this point, but I was making it. I was reminded of a movie that fascinated me as a kid - (one I really shouldn't have been watching), the "Working Girl". *Don't worry, not that kind of working girl.* This movie actually helped shape my vision of wanting to work in corporate America. It was the story of a woman who moved from a small town to a big city and backed her way into a high-end career as a business woman. She didn't earn it in the traditional way through college, but proved her intelligence with experience and rocked it!

Well – here I found myself at 22 years old suited up and sitting on the stairs of a major financial institution in the traffic filled streets of Downtown Chicago. I was waiting to start my first day as an Investment professional. I couldn't believe it! How did I get here! I admit I had to work harder and more persistent than most, but I did it! I went from starting in an entry-level position of a predominantly white male field, to being one of the only women of color promoted to the leadership team. I had now become a big girl in a big city, but secretly fighting a small town mentality.

The Secret is Out!

What happens when your favorite purse breaks? You know when you're out and the zipper stops zipping or the strap breaks way. You are now left to figure out what to do! That cute over the arm bag quickly turns into a clutch! Or you are left holding the purse manually together to protect the contents from falling out.

Well, as I've evolved over the years, I had to learn what to do in times like this. The honest answer is that I couldn't hold myself together when I was broken. I found myself trying to put me back together without success. When dark days approached and seemed to not go away, I had to dig deep in my bag to access a relationship that I grew distant from, my relationship with Jesus Christ. I remember being in a very low place in my twenties, even after the high of finding my identity in a new city. The things that I placed my confidence in such as love, money, and friendships, started disappointing me daily. I started losing my self-worth. In that small studio apartment I had days where I felt like my mind was at stake. The walls were closing in on me and the loneliness felt incredibly overwhelming. But then a SHIFT happened.

Every day I would come home and turn on my radio and hear a song that eventually would change the course of my walk with God. It was "Open up My Heart" by Yolanda Adams. I grew to love it and every time I turned my radio on desiring to hear the words that encouraged having a conversation with God, it would be on! I mean every time! As soon as I entered the house or the car... it would play. It was a little eerie at first, but I then realized the Lord wanted my attention for real.

My life was shifting and I was truly learning to lean on the Lord. Because my mother kept us in church all my life, I was no stranger to God. But, what I had not yet learned to do was walk with him daily for myself. It was my conversations with Him that got me through the dark days and literally pulled me through. It was the strength of this relationship that would see me through the highs and lows of the years to come.

It was God who met me in the painful breakup of my long-term relationship that later resulted in a long-term marriage to the very same man. The man who has committed to building a life with me, the father of my children, and my greatest supporter - now 15 years and counting! HE was there in my joy of being a newlywed, and held me close through the trauma of miscarrying our first child. HE met me in the hard times of being separated from my Mom and sisters who live in Georgia; and gave me the forever bond I have with my sisters-in-love here in Chicago.

HE was there in the joy of delivering my babies I wasn't sure I'd be able to have, and through the painful loss of their Grandmother (Granny), my Spiritual Mother and Mother-in-Love. HE met me the day I openly confessed Him as my Lord and was there the day I became an Ordained Evangelist for His kingdom. HE was there when health issues impacted my body to the point of multiple surgeries, and He held my hand as I recovered from them all.

You see - I had no idea how to repair the broken pieces of my life or how I would carry them all without falling apart. They were sudden and unexpected like my broken purses. But one day, Jesus politely inserted Himself into the most important part of me, *my heart*. And since that day, I have been restored.

It was not many years later that I realized God wasn't done with just increasing my walk with Him, but He was drawing me closer to be used to pull others into this same walk. Something that little girl in her grandmother's kitchen NEVER saw for herself. But with the influence of a strong Mother that taught my sisters and me to love God early; a seed was planted. And as scripture says about Apostle Paul and Apollos, one planted, one watered, but it was God that gave the increase (1 Cor. 3:6).

I come from a beautiful family of strong women and men who love me and have helped shape who I am today. Dating back to my grandmother, I inherited their seeds of resilience, and on August 10th, 2002, my family multiplied when I married into a spiritually strong, loving, and dynamic family; "The Joneses." It is in this family, led by golden-hearted Pastors, that the seed of my faith was watered and bloomed! They showed me a different level of love for God and family. I never realized that the need to be raised, even as young adults in marriage, would be necessary, but it was. My husband and I have learned how to build our family through the help of our parents. With them I've grown into my roles as a wife, mother, professional and leader in the house of God. These titles describe the evolution of who I've become and now, the secret is out!

My Purse is continuously evolving and growing in her identity. She is more than just my secret keeper. She has gone from functional to fierce through the power of life's experiences under the shadow of God. I've embraced womanhood and have learned to accept all that God has placed inside of me. That young girl who loved to sit in Grandma's kitchen and watch her family share the secrets of their hearts, has now earned a seat at the table sharing a few secrets of her own.

Purse Prayer:

Lord – Thank you for being Lord over my life. It has been a journey and I realize Your hand has guided every step of the way. Thank you for the grace You give to all Your children and for Your willingness to hold onto me through my mistakes. Like my purse, I have chosen to carry You close and in my spirit. I pray that my life is one that reflects the multiple facets of who You are. I pray that anyone reading this book will experience joy and revelation about their own identity and cause them to reflect on where they've been in their journey. May they realize that it is in the exposure of our dark places that Your light has the ability to shine. Amen

(Psalms 27:1) The Lord is my light and my salvation, of whom shall I fear? the Lord is the strength of my life, of whom shall I be afraid.

FaLisa Ward-Jones

FaLisa Ward-Jones was born and raised in the great state of Omaha, Nebraska. She now resides in the suburbs of Chicago. Her greatest purpose has been the gift of having her children and building a strong, loving family with her husband of 15 years.

She is the wife of J. Quincy Jones, the love since her youth and greatest supporter. She is the mother of 4 beautiful children (Quentin, Teylor, Kyra, and Khalil).

When FaLisa said yes to the Lord, He elevated her to become an Ordained Evangelist. She has spent the last 13 years of her life committed to her ministry work of preaching and teaching the Word of God to children and families bringing them closer to Christ.

She is the President of the True Foundation Church women's ministry and works with her husband serving over the youth ministry.

FaLisa knows that everyday she is evolving into the woman God has intended for her to be. This has carried into her professional life as well. FaLisa began college at the University of Nebraska- Lincoln. She decided to return to school and earned her A.S. Degree in Business from Colorado Technical University. She has earned multiple Investment security licenses and has been working for 17 years in the investment industry. FaLisa is Vice President at a large financial institute in Chicago, IL. and is highly skilled in the field of learning and development.

I Am...

A *Fierce* and *Fabulous* woman
who speaks life into those who encounter me.
I am on *Fire*.

~ DeYonne Parker ~

Chapter 4

Too Heavy a Load
By Chrystol Wilson-Payne

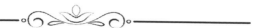

If my purse could talk it would say...

"She's missing out on the joy of the present because she's holding on to regret of the past and anxiety about the future. The weight is too heavy. I'm not sure how much longer we can hold it together.

Thanks to her mother, Chrystol started carrying a purse at a very early age. As a child, she carried me to church as an accessory to her frilliest Sunday dresses. I would hold tissue, mints and maybe a toy or two. I made her feel like a big girl. Chrystol was privileged to have a very happy childhood with very little to worry about. She had no burdens, concerns or emotional weight to carry. By her teenage years, she was carrying a purse daily. The contents changed as she began growing into a young woman. Instead of candy and tissue, she carried her favorite Bath and Body Works lotion, chapstick, lip gloss, a comb and whatever else she desired. I became a necessity but my contents were still light. As she transitioned to adulthood, my role changed. Once small, lightweight and cute, I became larger and filled with essentials; heavier with the weight of adulthood. Now that she's a wife and mother, I'm not sure who I belong to. Her life has become so full and complicated. She's trying so hard to carry it all with no complaints because she thinks she has to. Life has recently shown her that she can't can't control everything or handle it all on her own. Yet she continues to struggle to carry it all."

My Story

I'll start with a statement of truth about myself. My name is Chrystol and I despise making mistakes and have a fear of failure. Planning, goal setting and control tend to be my chosen methods to achieve success in life and reduce my anxiety about the future. As a teenager and young adult, I didn't allow myself to relax or get too comfortable. There was always a new goal to achieve.

I tried not to get weighed down by relationships. I was a military brat and moved every few years so I learned that the only thing consistent in life is change. Being this way served me well for most of my life but I had no idea how unprepared I was as I entered into one of the most difficult periods of my life.

About 18 months after we were married, my husband and I found out I was pregnant...SURPRISE! Well it wasn't really a surprise, but it wasn't necessarily planned like everything else in my life. It took me a few weeks to wrap my mind around the fact that this life changing event had occurred without planning. My plan was to be at my new job for a few years before having a child. I wanted to make the decision to have a child not just have it happen. I didn't feel ready. I cried and cried and cried some more. Then I wiped my tears and went back to what I knew to do; research and plan. I did all the research I could on pregnancy and tried to plan out the next 9 months.

At 8 weeks, we went to our first obstetrics appointment for an ultrasound. That's when we found out we were having twins! I handled the news that I was pregnant with twins much better than the news that I was pregnant. I literally laughed out loud when the doctor said "There's two!" I felt like I had been blessed with a very special experience and the bonus was that required so much planning (my favorite). I was going to be the best mother EVER. The moment I gave birth to my daughters, my life changed forever. It's hard to put into words what it felt like to become the mother of two in an instant. All I can say is that who I was before their birth no longer existed. The woman that left with two babies was someone with no identity outside of mommy.

It felt like a part of me died so my daughters could live in my heart and fill it with this overwhelmingly beautiful and painful love for them. The weight of new motherhood was tremendous. Although the first few months of twin parenthood were a blur, things went pretty smoothly, until one of my daughters suffered a severe injury. The injury was the result of what was supposed to be simple surgery on my 4 month old baby girl's pinky finger. She had surgery to remove a small skin tag from her pinky finger. Six days after the surgery she lost the first joint of her left ring finger. I will never forget the moment I realized something was wrong. I unwrapped her bandage and saw the damage to her little hand. She cried in pain. I fell to the floor, sobbing and screaming "What did they do to my baby?!"

It felt like my whole world crumbled around me in one moment. I was so confused. How could that happen to my baby? I had spent so much of my life devoting time, energy and love to other people's children and this is what happened to *my* child. I was taught that whatever you sow, you will reap. So why was this happening? I have sown good seed for years and this is what I reap?

It made NO SENSE AT ALL! It felt like a sick joke. For the first month or so, I prayed that I'd wake up and it would all be a nightmare. Nope. It was real. I woke up every single day, looked at her hand and saw that it was real. All of the hope I had for my future and her future was gone. Most of the hope and faith I had in God was gone too. It's amazing how your outlook on life can shift with just one event.

Remember when I said I have a fear of failure? Well that's what I saw this as... the biggest failure of my life. In fact, I told myself I was a failure every day. I kept remembering a moment I had with my daughter before the surgery when I looked into her big brown eyes and said "I won't let anything bad happen to you." I failed her...miserably. I suffered from severe depression and anxiety for about a year after her injury. No one knew how low I really was.

There were days I simply didn't want to wake up and face a life filled with guilt, shame and regret. My life felt so heavy I didn't feel like I had the strength to bear it. But I kept waking up. I believed I'd be even more of a failure if I let anyone know how depressed I was.

I tried my best to give the appearance of good mental health. At the same time, I decided that I could not allow myself to be happy until I knew for certain that my daughter would be happy despite her injury. How could I smile, knowing that one day people might point and stare at her? How could I forgive myself without knowing if she would forgive me? How could I simply move on when I felt so much anger and disappointment in myself? Truthfully, I wasn't only mad at myself. I was so angry at God. How could He allow this? I was taught that "God won't put more on you than you can handle" and "...we know all things work together for good to them that love God..."(Romans 8:28 NKJV). Well, I couldn't handle what happened and I didn't see any good coming from it! I was so angry. I was sad. I was disappointed. I was confused. I was lost. I was alone. I was hopeless. I carried all of those emotions in my heart...my broken heart, and I didn't think anyone knew. But that kind of despair cannot stay hidden for long.

All of those feelings came to the surface at my daughters' first birthday party. I tried my best to appear to be in a celebratory mood, but the truth was that I felt like a pressure cooker. I woke up angry. I should have been thinking about celebrating my daughters' first year of life but I was thinking about how much of a failure my first year of parenthood had been. I was pushing through and trying my best to be happy. Then a stranger came into my space and said the wrong thing. I lost it. I had never lost my temper in such a way. All of the anger I had built up in those 8 months was released on that person. I really don't know everything I said and did but I know I've never reacted in that way before. After the situation calmed down, I went to the bathroom to compose myself. I looked in the mirror and didn't recognize the woman looking back at me. When I came out, I looked into the eyes of those around me and I knew they could now see how broken I was. I also knew I could no longer force myself to live with that pain but I had no idea what to do with it. We went on with the party that day with only a brief mention of what had occurred. I don't think anyone really knew what to say or how to help me. This was unfamiliar territory for everyone.

A few weeks later, my husband and I attended a new members' class for the church we joined. The leader of the group asked if there was anything that was keeping us from having a closer relationship with God. We were told to write it down on a card. I struggled with telling the truth or just giving a good church answer. The Holy Spirit said "Just write it Chrystol." So I did. "I'm angry at myself and at God..." Then the leader of the group asked if anyone wanted to share. Before I knew it, my hand was raised. I know a shackle was broken the moment I raised my hand.

I openly shared my true, raw feelings for the first time. I couldn't believe I was telling a room full of strangers how I felt but I'm so glad I did. The leader said "It wasn't your fault Chrystol. The enemy wants you to believe God doesn't love you but He does. That's why you're here right now." She told me to stand up and had everyone surround me. They all gathered around me and prayed for me. I wept as they surrounded me with love and petitioned God to heal my heart and mind. I could only release that pain by giving it a voice. I had to tell the truth. That was the first step in my healing process.

The next step in my process was releasing my need for answers. I kept asking myself and God the question why?

Would knowing why really help me move forward? No! There was no good, logical or acceptable answer to that question. So I needed to shift my focus from why to what now? A terrible thing happened. I couldn't change the past and didn't know what would happen in the future.

I had to forgive myself and stop holding myself hostage to that one decision. In the process of forgiving myself, I realized that what was causing me so much anxiety was fear that my daughter would blame me and feel like I failed her. I was afraid that the bond and love I shared with her would one day be destroyed.

Graciously, God gave me the gift of a spiritual retreat called the Encounter. I was given the opportunity to ask someone I had hurt or wronged for forgiveness. A woman stood in proxy as my daughter and I was able to ask her forgiveness for making the wrong decision. This woman knew nothing about me or my daughter, but the Holy Spirit gave her the words to say to me (as my daughter) and in that moment, I was free of those anxious thoughts.

My healing process has not been easy but I've felt God's love for me through it all. The process involved prayer, therapy and allowing other people to help me.

No matter the hurt, there are certain steps necessary for healing.

- Acknowledge or admit the injury
- Locate the pain and give it sound
- Take it to the Father & surrender control
- Receive His comfort and correction
- Allow the pain to mature you
- Learn and apply new insight & revelation

God has shown me that the life I hope for is still possible. My daughter is thriving. She's so confident. Most of the time, she's fine with having a "special" finger. Of course I wish none of it had ever happened, but it did. I accept it now and I can leave it in the past. I now know that dark moments, setbacks, and failures don't need to be avoided (they can't be anyway). My faith has never been stronger. I am at peace with what happens in my life because I truly believe Romans 8:28: "And we know that all things work together for good to them that love God, to them who are the called according to his purpose."

There was beauty in the broken pieces of my heart, but it could only manifest by giving them to God. Instead of carrying all of my burdens, I give them to Jesus. I hope you've been encouraged to open your purse to expose the broken pieces of your heart and the burdens you try to carry alone. One of the benefits of living for Jesus is that His yoke is easy and his burden is light. My life isn't supposed to feel heavy because it's in His hands. I'm still a planner, but the plan I'm most dependent on is God's plan.

Purse Prayer:

Heavenly Father,

When I find myself weighed down by my life, I thank You that Your Word says "Take my yoke upon you, and learn of me; for I am meek and lowly in heart: and ye shall find rest unto your souls. For my yoke is easy, and my burden is light." (Matthew 11:29 -30) Thank You for showing me that I was not created to carry the weight of life all by myself. When I accepted You into my heart, I gained access to Your grace, strength and wisdom. Your grace does not give me the power to do everything. It gives me power to do everything you've called me to do. It is not by my own strength, knowledge and planning that I achieve success. There is so much peace in surrendering my plans to You; knowing that You will endow me with all I need to fulfill my purpose. I pray that every woman reading this book experiences that same peace.

In Jesus' Name, Amen.

Chrystol Wilson - Payne

Chrystol Wilson-Payne, is a tenured Licensed Professional Counselor. For 10+ years, she has worked with individuals, couples, groups and families. She is a devoted wife to her college sweetheart, Kevin and proud mother of twin daughters Morgan & Kyndall.

She is an active member of her church where she serves as Deacon and ministry leader.

Chrystol's passion is to challenge, encourage and empower women and girls to become the best version of themselves.

She does this professionally through her work as a therapist in private practice as well as providing tips and inspiration on her Facebook & Instagram pages under the name *The Curly Counselor*. She also shares personal experiences and insights in her blog *Journey to Better* along with other online publications. She volunteers her time as a mentor, board member and Girl Scout troop leader.

Her passion project is the quarterly #IMatter challenge that she created to inspire women to do one small thing each day to practice self-care.

Chapter 5

Opening Up A Can Of Worms!
By Alicia J. Ward

The sanctity of a woman's purse transcends the generations of women who have gone on before me. The sacredness of a woman's purse surpasses not only the material it is made out of but also the name brand that has often been associated with stature. A woman's purse has long been thought of literally as a "NO MANS" land; a bottomless pit of sorts, that appears to be equipped to hold everything but the kitchen sink. In reality, a women's purse holds more than just the material trappings of life; it holds a significance and connotation that means more than one could ever dare to envision.

The most commonly used definition of the word PURSE, defined by the Encarta English Dictionary is a "woman's bag for carrying everyday belongings." Through further examination, a PURSE can also be defined and associated with the non-bag type such as a boxer's purse which is the "PRIZE money awarded at a sporting event." Upon combining the two definitions, I have created a new meaning: "A PURSE is a woman's bag used for carrying her

PRIZED possessions and do not get it twisted; she will fight you like a BOXER if you go into it without her permission!" There you have it.

I can remember as a child growing up, God forbid, if my siblings and I dared to cross the line and venture into the abyss of our mother's purse; uninvited. JESUS! Looking back, according to her reaction, you would have thought we just killed someone! I can still hear my mother's voice now, *"Didn't I tell you not to go into my purse without asking?"* My mother also told us repeatedly, not to drink out of her glass. I can recall one day that I unknowingly swallowed a mouthful of something that nearly burned a hole in my throat; I finally understood. My hard-headedness gave her the opportunity to use yet another one her motherly colloquialisms, *"That will teach you to listen!"* Nevertheless, I learned a valuable lesson, "Always sniff what is in the glass before you drink out of it!" What does one have to do with the other? The purse and glass are metaphors of life that represents the privacy and boundaries that are often crossed when we do not honor or respect the wishes of others. My siblings and I were guilty as charged. Even still, I can remember thinking to myself, what is in that purse? What was she hiding from us? As children, we let our imaginations run wild. The possibility that our mom was living a double life and working as a spy was always on the forefront of our minds, because of the secrecy of that purse!

The suspense would almost kill us until one day, on my own, I was certain that I may never solve the mystery of the purse and I would just have to be okay with that. After all, I resolved that respecting my mother's boundaries and her right to privacy was much more important.

In retrospect, I was such a tomboy growing up that I was really not into purses , that is, not until I was forced to carry one due to *Mother Nature*, if you know what I mean. As if, this unwanted visitation was not bad enough, now I had to carry a purse too! Oh the humiliation! When will it end? Such is the life of a teenage girl, so much drama! To make matters worse, back in my day we did not have many options when it came to our unwanted "monthly visitor." Unlike today, compact items that a woman could discreetly carry in her pocket were not an option. During that particular "time of the month," carrying a purse was necessary however; the purse had to be the size of a small overnight bag. You felt like the entire school knew why you were carrying that suitcase of a purse, all of a sudden. I am exaggerating a little. Because I associated purses with the feeling of embarrassment, I never wanted to carry one.

When asked to collaborate on this project, I felt compelled to open up a can of worms which was sealed past the expiration date. As cliché as this may be, every woman's purse serves as the container where she hides the difficult to face, complex issues of her life. Any attempt to examine the contents can potentially cause her to face the reality of her own vulnerabilities. Her purse is the one place where she has complete control. Her purse speaks of her insecurities. Her purse speaks of her fears. Her purse speaks of her pain. Her purse speaks of her sadness. Her purse speaks of her successes. Her purse speaks of her failures. Her purse speaks of her triumphs. Her purse speaks of her joy. Her purse resonates with a voice that only she can hear.

When it speaks, it can echo a sense of tranquility in a world that is full of noise or it can reflect a sense of insecurity in a world that demands perfection. Ironically, I finally understand how my mother felt.

What's in my purse?

When I began to give this issue serious thought, what immediately came to mind was that globally successful credit card commercial, when the spokesperson asks us that one important question, *"What's in your wallet?"* I could not help but to chuckle to myself, because I know in those moments when I feel uncomfortable, I use my sense of humor as a defense mechanism. Why do I feel uncomfortable? What am I afraid the contents of my purse will reveal about me to the world?

The answer hit me; it is usually during my most uncomfortable moments that I become aware that God is preparing to propel me to the next level. In other words, God wants me to be comfortable enough to leave my purse unattended while I trust Him to watch it. This actually makes so much sense to me.

After experiencing one of the most difficult years of my life, I proclaimed that this would be my year of healing, facing truths, being transparent and trusting Him in all areas of my life. Be careful what you proclaim aloud, because God just might be listening. It does not matter whether you shout it from the mountaintops or if you whisper it softly, because God already knows your end before the beginning. Furthermore, once you know the truth, you are responsible for it. I am ready to face the truth of what my purse will reveal about me in this season of my life.

Upon examining my purse, at first glance it is a rather unassuming purse. Although my purse is a designer bag, it is still nothing fancy. This describes me to a fault! I have never considered myself to be a fashion forward person; in fact I prefer not to attract attention to myself if I can help it. It is not my objective to spend this time exposing the meaning behind the items found in most purses. Instead, I am choosing to understand why I am holding on to specific items in my purse. The first couple of items that immediately caught my eyes are the programs from my brother's memorial and my dad's funeral. I was not kidding when I previously mentioned that I had a difficult year. Imagine, losing your brother and father within three months. My brother and my dad were the first two men in my life that I ever loved and now they are gone. Carrying around their programs, are a constant reminder of how precious life is and the importance of appreciating family.

Next, I found a handful of coupons stuffed in the back pocket of my purse; some were still good and some were expired. You are probably thinking to yourself, how could a bunch of old coupons, possibly be related to something profound and deep about my life? That is what I thought, but then, I received a coupon revelation one night when I could not sleep. Just in case you did not know, the Holy Spirit is always awake and ready to give you revelation at any time. You just have to be ready and willing to listen whenever he speaks. The coupons represent the fact, that I often undervalue and sell short my gifts, talents and worth. I thought to myself, no one, but the Holy Spirit, can get this deep about coupons! This revelation hurt, but it is accurate. After all, I can recall numerous times, that a potential client inquired about utilizing my services and before you know it, I was offering the "friends and family" discount. The coupons current and expired, revealed to me that I do not often place value on my own gifts which can be translated to mean that I am not confident enough to charge what God says I am worth. Why do I do this? After careful consideration, I realized that for much too long, I allowed corporate America to place a value on my gifts and talents, which determined the corporate bottom line. Of course, the monetary value did not align with the qualifications and experience that I brought to the table. As a result, even as an entrepreneur, I continue to diminish my own self-worth by relying on worldly measures instead of kingdom standards. You know what this means, NO MORE COUPONS, the sale is over!

Finally, I cannot help but to notice the silver business card holder. I ordered it after my layoff in 2012. It bares the inscription, *There is Life After Layoff*® which is the inspiration and God ordained vision behind my life's journey. My purpose is to share that our job is only what we do and not who we are. After the job ends, it is time to start living the life that God intends for us to live. We are all here for a reason; there are no accidental lives, but it is up to us to discover our "WHY?". The holder and the business cards inside of it, remind me that God has a plan for my life. He proclaims this in Jeremiah 29:11: "For I know the plans I have for you" declares the Lord, "plans to prosper you and not to harm you, plans to give you a hope and a future." The beauty in all of this is that, He revealed His plan for my life in the midst of, what some might call, a devastating life-altering event. The scripture Romans 8:28 relates to this directly when it says: "And we know that God causes all things to work together for good to those who love God, to those who are called according to His purpose." Now ask yourself, "Who is God calling me to be?"

What happened next was totally unexpected. While continuing to survey the contents of my purse, an overwhelming feeling of emptiness, suddenly came over me. It was in that moment, that I realized that my purse was actually "EMPTY" and void of life despite its contents. I can see your face, head leaned to one side, eyes squinted, as you do your best *"What you talking about Willis?"* impression! I was just like you, I did not understand either, but then the Holy Spirit revealed to me how this is a direct correlation to my life.

Outside of the essentials, such as my wallet (which carries my driver's license, money, and debit cards etc.), my cell phone, headphones and a few other small miscellaneous items, my purse invokes a feeling of sadness and even possesses a feeling of numbness.

This spoke volumes to me and if I am honest, it even shook me up a little, because, as much as I hate to admit, this revelation is on point with where I am emotionally in this season of my life. I am pretty sure that the sadness and numbness that I am feeling, has everything to do with the recent losses of my father and brother, which has even left me feeling a sense of loneliness in my season of grieving.

I feel alone, because until you have personally experienced a similar type of loss, you cannot possibly understand my pain. However, my willingness to embrace the pain and loneliness while I start the long journey towards healing, has guided me to finding a support group that can understand what I feel and this has helped me tremendously. One of the first things that we were told is that grief is a process and that it is not a sign of weakness, it is a sign of being human, and it is the cost of loving someone. First, you have to give yourself permission to grieve. Permission granted.

I must admit, that the process of looking into the purse of my life has been a little painful but also very therapeutic. This is a perfect example of how our pain is often a teacher. Pain is something that can be used to pull from us when all else fails. It made me realize, that the burdens we carry or hold onto, will not bring us happiness and can ultimately hold us back from all God created us to be.

Furthermore, how can we relate this to our walk with God? He is not interested in what we have accumulated materially in this life; which means that we should not be either. After all, materialism or seeking to have things is a form of idolatry and not pleasing to God. In Colossians 3:2, scripture tells us to "Set your affection on things above, not on things on the Earth." Our goal should be to seek a close personal relationship with Him.

At this point, you may be wondering, what my revelations has to do with what God revealed to me through the contents of my purse. My purse is the container of my life.

Through the examination of its contents, I have come to realize, that I need to work on my relationship with God and submit to Him the areas of my life that concern me. My starting point is the expectations that I may have set for the people with whom I am in relationship with and how I should not rely on them to make me happy. Next, I am responsible for my own happiness and if I settle for being in the company of other people, instead of in the presence of God, I am selling myself short. Furthermore, my purse revealed to me that I should not allow myself to be fascinated with the material trappings of this world in addition to what people may think or say about me. I am worthy of love and created on purpose for a purpose.

One thing I know for sure, God will never have to ask my permission to go into my life's purse!

Purse Prayer:

Heavenly Father,

Thank you for going into my purse without permission to show me the contents of my heart through the contents of my purse, may I find comfort in your Word and revelation; guide me in letting go of any expectations of people that I have and my reliance on STUFF to make me happy; help me to submit to You the things that concern me as I grow in relationship with You; help fill any void that I feel with the purpose and plan that you have ordained for my life. Lord I am grateful for your conviction as I grow and learn from the pain in my life; help me to embrace the journey; help me to heal as I continue to give myself permission to grieve the losses that I have endured and not feel condemned or guilty about what I may or may not have done in those relationships; Lord, help me to forgive those who have hurt me and may I show them the same grace and forgiveness that you have shown me. Father I am grateful for this season of HARVEST; continue to show me the WHY of my purpose; reveal to me the relationships that I need to let go of and allow them to blow off of the windshield of my life; guide me into healthy relationships with people of purpose. Lord allow me to have discernment in both my personal and professional relationships and guide me in being able to use my gifts and talents to invoke positive change and be a blessing in the lives of others.

In your darling son Jesus' name I pray – AMEN

Alicia Ward

Alicia Ward is a wife and mother of two adorable children, who resides in Metro Atlanta. She attended and graduated Cum Laude from the historically renowned Tuskegee University with a Bachelor of Science degree in Business Administration. After graduating from Tuskegee, Alicia pursued her professional career in Atlanta, as a Commercial Production Underwriter. It was while working in this capacity, that Alicia encountered her first experience of a layoff.

It was a long and challenging road, to get back on her feet, and one that left her feeling broken and with low self-esteem. As life oftentimes repeats itself, Alicia found herself once again apart of a major company layoff from her job of almost fourteen years.

As a result, Alicia's blog *There is Life After Layoff*® was born. The success of the blog resulted in her hosting a talk radio show of the same name. In addition, she is also the author of *There is Life After Layoff-Rediscovery and Empowerment Journal,* as well as a motivational speaker and business coach.

I Am...

A *Confident* and courageous woman
boldly moving towards the *Dreams*
God placed inside of me

~ DeYonne Parker ~

Chapter 6

Put Me Down and Free My Carrier

(I'm tired, retired and ready to be free)
By Carol J. Harvey

When my carrier was asked to answer the question, "If her purse could talk, what would it say?" it stirred up a lot of things inside her. First, let me start out by introducing you to my carrier. Her name is Carol Harvey. She's the mother of three beautiful girls, LaShonda Warley, DeYonne Parker and FaLisa Jones. She has two bonus children from her current marriage, Christopher Harvey and Kristian Wilson and is the proud grandmother to 11 grandchildren. My carrier is affectionately known as Mama Carol to those she mentors and to anyone who may need a motherly touch at any given time. Although she's retired from a 15 year career in the field of nursing, she still cares very much about the well-being of others.

"Who am I?" you ask. Well, I'm Bella, her bright, bodacious bag. Yep, her pretty, poised purse! But, we weren't always this way. As you read this chapter, you'll discover that my carrier, Carol, and I have been through a lot together...three husbands, life as a single mom, holding down two jobs to raise 3 daughters and a rollercoaster ride through trials and triumphs. I hide all her secrets, carry all her emotions and hold all her junk. I guess you can say, I'm her best friend.

My carrier and I started "life" together very young. I was little, cute, round, colorful, and stylish and was toted around everywhere she went. I held all of her lively life possessions! Carol was sassy and jazzy and so was I! She laughed and smiled a lot and was always curious about what life had to offer her. I was full of stuff that brought her joy! Our journey started to shift when Carol, at the age of 17 married husband number 1...yep, she was young, dumb and in love. Too young to know any better, baby number 1 came soon after she turned 18. Over the course of 9 months, my carrier began to grow physically and so did I. *Life was starting to change.*

Soon after her first child, her marriage to husband number 1 started to fade. Happiness was slowly sifting to the bottom of me and fear and sadness surfaced to the top. My carrier was starting to mature. She changed me, I was bigger and my content was different. A diaper, baby bottle and pacifier fell in with fear, hurt, sadness, and happiness deep in the bottom of me, but determination was moving to the top. My carrier was determined to take care of herself and baby number 1, and she did just that. Living in a place of her own and caring for her baby, she was maturing.

A couple of years later came husband number 2 and a short time later baby number 2. Happiness returned to the top and I became sturdier, still had my style and color but junk was slowly filtering in. *Life was changing; my carrier was maturing.*

A big life change came along and we left home and traveled to the state of California. During our stay here, baby number 3 arrived. Throughout the time we were living in a new state, I changed many times and then I was accompanied by a larger bag called a diaper bag for baby number 3. We were all doing well and happiness was still at the top of me, but, I was getting pretty full. My carrier had a lot of other emotions starting to show up.

Carol and husband number 2 began to experience turbulence in their marriage. Secrets were starting to fall into me like a tube of lipstick falling straight to the bottom. Happiness was turning into confusion, deceit, and sadness. Determination was still there, but somewhere stuck in in between sadness and happiness. Although my carrier was experiencing a lot of emotions, she would still put on her happy face for her daughters. I knew it was a mask; one she was determined to wear every day for the sake of her girls.

One day tragedy struck my carrier and husband number 2 and their lives were changed forever. Baby number 3 was burned very badly by someone she trusted to care for her baby. This shook my carrier to her core. She lived for her babies, and to know she couldn't protect her baby lead to guilt and shame; two new emotions that fell in amongst all the others that I was carrying. *Life was changing.*

After caring for baby number 3, my carrier and husband number 2 decided to move back to Nebraska for the sake of their babies.

Determination grew stronger, but happiness was still at the bottom and confusion, pain and hurt were slowly fading. Sadness was still there but not as prevalent. I was beginning to feel a little lighter, something was happening, I hadn't been changed I was still big and sturdy. I had a lot to hold. Fear was still lurking around trying very hard to surface to the top, but guilt and shame were on the bottom.

Finally, we made it back home. My carrier was happy! I felt her fear sinking, her confidence just popped up out of nowhere, it was like she was on a mission. Life was changing my carrier was maturing we were growing. Unfortunately, husband number 2 didn't make it with us. The trials that they faced in their marriage were too great for my carrier to handle. So, she moved on with her 3 daughters. *Life was changing.*

The girls started growing, spreading their wings and becoming more active. My carrier wanted to make things work for them, so she began working two jobs to provide the things they needed. Every morning she would leave with me on one side and her gym/work bag on the other. She didn't have time to come home before heading to her next job, so she packed everything she needed.

My carrier was very torn about working two jobs. This meant she had to be away from her girls a lot and had to trust them to take care of each other. The two oldest girls were teens, but the youngest was only seven. She was very worried about her, because there were times she was at home alone. It was only an hour, but for THAT little one, that was a long time.

As time went on, my carrier grew into her new normal and seemed to be feeling better about how everything was going. Her confidence was back, determination was floating on top, and unwanted junk sunk to the bottom. She had matured. As a single mom, working two jobs was not easy. She was very busy and constantly on the move, but always had her girls in mind. Before we left the house each morning, she would leave strict instructions for each one of the girls to complete before she returned home.

The two older girls were told to come straight home from school to be there with the younger one. The oldest, LaShonda, who was only 12, was responsible for cooking for the other two. My carrier was very weighed down by this; she hated putting that responsibility on her oldest child; more guilt sifting down to the bottom of me.

She stood strong and tough in front of her girls and had all the kids in the neighborhood thinking she was hard core. When those kids would see her car coming they would all scatter. But I knew her well and all that she felt. Once she was in the car she would cry and ask God to watch over her babies, cover and protect them while she was away from them. *Life was changing.*

My carrier continued to work hard, but also found a little time to party when she could. Her confidence was back and strong. The girls were old enough to leave alone at night for a while. So, sometimes we would hit the clubs and go shake our groove thang! She started dating a little, but would never let the girls see who she was seeing because she was very cautious about who she allowed to enter their lives.

Time was moving on. My carrier was taking care of things. She pushed a lot of stuff down in me, but was determined to keep moving forward. All her dark secrets had filtered down to the bottom. Determination and confidence were at the top. So, we were doing ok, but once again, *life was changing.*

One day, my carrier and the girls were home watching TV, something they did often, and a news alert concerning husband number 2 flashed across the TV. A picture of his face appeared on the screen and the news reported that he had been arrested for arm robbery. The girls were shocked! This was their father. They hadn't seen a lot of him since he and my carrier divorced, but they desperately tried to keep in touch with him. So, this was a hard blow for them. Their father...in jail. It was especially hard for DeYonne. She loved her daddy so much, they all did, but she was the closest to him. She tried so hard to be with him, but he would never return her calls or come see her. Still, she never gave up on him.

My carrier had buried all the love and feelings she had for husband number 2. There was nothing in her heart for him, but she became very angry with him because she knew the pain he was causing their daughters. And yet again, she would have to pick up the pieces. To her surprise, husband number 2 was sentenced to serve time in prison.

She had several discussions with the girls to attempt to explain their father's behavior. The last thing she wanted was for her daughters to carry the guilt of what he did, or blame themselves for his actions. These conversations were hard and hurtful, but necessary.

As time went on, so did the girls. They wrote their father a few times and he wrote back as well, but the letters became fewer and fewer. He even wrote my carrier, but she never wrote him back. *Life was changing.*

About 4 years after the devastating news of husband number 2 going to prison, my carrier got a phone call no one ever should receive. It was husband number 2's sister. She tearfully explained to my carrier that husband number 2, the father of her children, had died in prison. The prison officials legally declared it was suicide. For the first time, in a very long time, all the hidden emotions my carrier thought she buried deep inside of me, started to resurface. She didn't know how to feel. Sadness, sorrow, hurt, and anger, all started rushing up and spilling over. I heard my carrier say, "How am I going to tell my girls?", "How do I tell them their father is dead?". My carrier decided to tell her oldest and youngest daughter first. They cried so hard. I felt so much sadness from my carrier for her girls. She knew the hardest thing was going to be telling DeYonne. She still held hope for a relationship with her father, even though she hadn't heard from him in a long while. Her love for him was strong. They had an unbreakable bond.

So, with a tremble in her voice, my carrier told her baby girl that her Daddy had died. And she had to watch her baby crumble to the ground and hear her scream, "I knew something was wrong. I dreamt it Mama!". My carrier's heart was broken and now regret had flowed in, along with guilt and sadness. She wished she had done a better job with telling her girls about the loss of their father.

It took a while, but eventually, the girls accepted the loss of their father and started moving forward with their lives. My carrier moved on also, but she was still wearing the mask for her girls. She kept all the junk pushed down inside of me. *Life was changing.*

Once again, my carrier found a little time to go out and enjoy herself. After all she had been through, she truly deserved a few moments of freedom. On one occasion we got dressed up and went out with her favorite cousin to one of their usual hanging spots. This is where she met Leon. He was a very kind and thoughtful man and appeared to be different than the others. She had been shielding herself for a long time, but I suddenly felt a spark of light shoot from her heart. Leon and my carrier began dating and she was happy.

We had a lot of time with Leon. He traveled quite a bit, which worked for my carrier's lifestyle. She had time for her girls and when Leon would come into town, she spent time with him too. Their relationship went on for 6 years and my carrier experienced both joy and pain during this period. *Life was changing.*

During their 6 years of dating, the worst thing that could've happen...happened! My carrier got pregnant. One of her worst fears! She was very angry with herself. "How could she let this happen?" she thought. She consistently spoke about unprotected sex and pregnancy with the girls. She was teaching them that their bodies were a treasure. Now, here she was facing this unthinkable situation. One that she never thought she would be in at this time in her life.

In a desperate attempt to maintain her determined effort to care for her 3 daughters, my carrier did something she thought she'd never do - she had an abortion. She felt she had no choice at the time. So much guilt and shame flooded in and sunk to the bottom of my inner lining. A deep sadness fell over my carrier, but once again, she put on her mask and moved forward. Her relationship with Leon was fading fast. She had to make some changes in their relationship for the sake of her girls. They discussed their future and the possibility of marriage. She wanted her daughters to know that being in the *right* loving relationship should lead to marriage.

Leon decided that he wasn't ready for this type of commitment and was fine with the way things were at the time. My carrier was devastated because she knew she had to do something that would cause her more pain - let him go. So she did and it nearly broke her. Here we were again, pain, hurt, confusion, all resurfaced to the top of me. How much more could she take? Every time she moved forward something would drastically happen that would push her backwards again.

She found herself at a crossroad. *Life was changing.*

My carrier had always believed in God, but she would tell

Him she didn't need him right now because she had it all together but this time was different. She knew she was at the end of her rope.

Life felt as if it was over and everything was broken within her. My carrier desperately needed Him NOW!

As I sat on the corner of her dresser, the place where she always put me, my carrier fell to her knees and pressed her face to the ground and began crying uncontrollably. She vulnerably cried out to God, which is something she hadn't done in a while. I heard her say: *"Lord, please forgive me for my sins. Please forgive me for having an abortion. Thank You for allowing me to send my baby back to You. Forgive me Father for all my sins and I will follow You Lord. If there is anyone out there for me Lord, I know You will bring them to me. I will no longer be searching for that person. I trust You, Lord. Please help me to go on Father. Take this pain from my heart and let me move forward for my girls. I ask You this in the name of Jesus – Amen"*

Then she took a big sigh and released it; got up off her knees, dried her tears, put her mask on and went out to talk with her girls about all that had happened. *Life was changing. My carrier had surrendered.*

As Carol and I started moving forward, the contents she was putting inside of me were changing. One day a little book, called the Bible, was placed inside me on top of all the junk. She and the girls were going to church a lot more. She kept little cards with prayers on them inside me. She had prayers on her dresser and everywhere she could put them. My carrier wanted her girls to know and love God and to put Him first in their lives. She knew that one day they would stray away from Him, but wanted to plant the seed deep inside so they would always return to Him.

Life was changing. Carol was feeling a little better about herself, but still had a lot of baggage hidden away in the bottom of my inner lining. She tried keeping determination and her confidence on top, but it was getting very hard because depression was trying to settle in with all the other junk.

I was becoming quite heavy. My carrier changed me to a big dull sturdy bag so I could hold all her junk. She was moving on, but still faking like everything was good. My carrier had accepted where she was at in her life and continued to navigate her path forward. This time with no expectations. So, what happened next completely caught her off guard. A co-worker stopped her in the hall at work and told her she had someone she wanted her to meet. The first thing that my carrier wanted to say was, "Hell NO!", but suddenly she opened her mouth and the words, "OK" flowed out. I think we were both surprised.

The co-worker arranged a meeting between the two of them and it was an immediate connection. I felt all of her emotions again. Hope, joy, and excitement resurfaced and made their way back up to the top. My carrier was still a bit hesitant, but I could feel her reimagining hope and happiness in her life. This time was different. She had stopped searching for love in her own efforts. This had to be a Holy hook-up because her hands were completely off of this encounter.

Jimmy Harvey entered her life and gave my carrier a new spark. These two talked EVERY DAY at work and on the phone to the wee hours of the night. They were like giddy teenagers. Her genuine smile returned and all the good stuff that found its way to the bottom of my inner lining, was rising to the top. All the other junk sank deeper and deeper to the bottom.

Things were going very well between Jimmy and Carol. So much so that my carrier made an intentional decision to introduce Jimmy and his children to her girls. They did everything together. Everyone seemed to be happy and they were officially a couple. *Life was changing!*

My carrier was feeling light and hopeful about her future. She was on her way to getting her happy ending! But, unfortunately, in the midst of her heart rediscovering love, an unexpected tragedy reared its ugly head again.

At 2AM, my carrier received a phone call from the hospital that no parent wants to receive. The person on the other end of the line began explaining that her two daughters had been badly hurt and that she should immediately come to the hospital. My carrier's worst fears had come true. She wasn't able to protect her babies. LaShonda and DeYonne were stabbed with a 6' inch butcher knife at the hands of LaShonda's abusive boyfriend. She knew he had hit LaShonda previously, which infuriated her and she warned him to never put his hands on her daughter again or there would be serious consequences. She never thought he would be crazy enough to hurt her daughter in this way.

The panic and fear in my carrier's heart rose to the top of me and spilled out. The thought of losing her girls was overwhelming. She snatched me up and we drove as fast as we could to get to her girls. When she arrived at the hospital, her heart sank even further when she laid eyes on them; there they were, hurt and in pain... something she had dreaded. LaShonda was covered in blood and her face was so swollen from the beating she took. DeYonne was also covered with blood from her injuries and hysterical from all she had experienced that night. My carrier was in a state of shock and disbelief and wondered how this could have happened to her girls! Both girls had surgery to repair the injuries they suffered and when they returned home my carrier never left their side.

Carol was so grateful that she had Jimmy in her life. He was right there with her and the girls. He comforted her and I could feel her letting him in. She felt completely protected when she was with him. All the fear and hurt she had inside started to fade, but guilt and shame were still lurking. Although the girls' physical wounds were starting to heal, she worried about how they would thrive later in life.

The girls had to face their abuser one more time. This time it was in a court room. The abuser was found guilty and sentenced to 15 consecutive years in prison for the hurt and pain he caused. This was a huge relief to my carrier to know that he was no longer a threat to her girls. *Life was changing.*

My carrier and her girls moved forward. Happiness started to return and their lives were changed. She began to see all that God had done and was continuing to do in her life. All the pain and sorrow she went through led her to this moment. She remembered the prayer she prayed and God answered her in a mighty way. He not only healed her hurt, took her family from broken to better, He also gave her the love of her life, Jimmy Harvey. *Her life was changing.*

Carol and Jimmy took the next big step in their relationship and got married! All their kids were there and excited to see their parents so in love and happy; I guess we could say they were soulmates. He was the YING to her YANG and the one she prayed for God to bring into her life.

My carrier's outlook on life changed and she started truly living again. The mask disappeared and she reconnected with her true and authentic self.

I changed too! I went from dull and sturdy to light weight, cute and colorful again. Hallelujah...I'm back! All the unwanted junk that sunk down to the bottom of me is finally gone.

My carrier is now retired and lives a very full life with her husband Jimmy Harvey. They have been married for 23 years and live comfortably in the state of Georgia. Carol's girls are now grown women with families of their own and they love God fiercely. She taught them well and from what I can see, they each have a bodacious bag they carry.

The look on my carrier's face represents the emotions that I now carry for her...joy, tranquility, excitement, love and of course happiness! We are back in stride again, but this time God is leading the way.

Life HAS changed!

Dear Heavenly Father, I thank You for Your grace and mercy. Thank You for the trials and tribulations you brought me through. Thank you Father for covering me and my family along the way. Putting You first in my life has made me the woman I am today and I praise and thank You, Father. I pray that my story will let every woman or man know that nothing is impossible through You. You are a way maker, a promise keeper and a light in the darkness. You brought me through my darkness and You never left me, I thank You, Lord. Life can be hard and sometimes unbearable. I have learned by putting you first in my life there is nothing I can't do. Thank you Heavenly Father I will praise and glorify You all the days of my life. In Jesus name – Amen.

Carol J. Harvey

Carol Harvey is a sassy, jazzy retiree. She is happily married to her soulmate, has three beautiful daughters she raised as a single parent and two bonus children from her current marriage.

One of Carol's biggest dreams was to be a nurse. She always believed and instilled in her daughters, that by putting God first in your life, there is nothing you can't do.

At the age of 47, through the encouragement of her family, and many prayers, she went to nursing school. Carol went to school during the day and worked at night. She struggled through school, she failed twice but never gave up.

Her determination paid off, she graduated from nursing school and became a Registered Nurse in Labor and Delivery for 15 years. Now enjoying her retirement, she mentors young girls and encourages them to always follow their dreams, trust and believe in God, and never give up.

I Am...

Open to receive all that is for me
and I *Welcome* the *evolution*
of my life's journey. I will not carry the weight
of trials that attempt to stand in my way.

~ DeYonne Parker ~

Chapter 7

~~Hidden~~ Discovered Treasure
By DeYonne Parker

Welcome to the contents of my sassy satchel. Yep...that's what I call my purse, along with some other fun names you'll soon find out in this chapter.

So, who am I? Well, I'm glad you asked! The name I was given at birth is DeYonne Parker. Since then it has evolved into "Dee" and other names have been attached to it which make-up the sum of who I am. Those names include, Mr. Parker's best friend, mother of 2 handsome young men, 1/3 of Carol Jean's daughters, sister, friend, published author, personal empowerment coach, business partner, visionary and compiler of "If Her Purse Could Talk", founder of The S.W.A.G. University and multi-national speaker & facilitator.

Whew! Now that we've gotten that out of the way, let me say that all those names simply mean is that I'm walking in my God-given purpose and I'm forever grateful to our Heavenly Father. It means that I've acknowledged that God has plans for me and I've accepted the challenge to be stretched; and I do mean STRETCHED!

After writing my first book, *Girl, Get Your S.W.A.G. Back! - A Soul-Freeing Journey for Women,* I thought I had unpacked all the difficult situations in my life. I mentally revisited the scene where the man that abused my sister, stabbed me with a 6-inch butcher knife. I gave up the mask I was hiding behind and stopped fakin', foolin' and frontin'. I confronted the pain of my past and exposed the areas where I lost my **Self-confidence**, my **Walk with God**, my **Attitude of Gratitude** and my **God-given Gifts and Talents**. At that time, I figured God had sifted through my life, purged my soul, laid it out for others to find their healing through my story and now I was done. Right? Wrong!

Apparently, there's still more of me that God wants poured out into books, blogs and broadcasts. So, here I am...challenged with providing an authentic answer to the provocative question that I've asked others to answer; *"If your purse could talk, what would it say?"*

After many, MANY, real and emotional conversations with myself and God about how to launch this project, I'm now ready to dig deep again and share my truth. What better way to unravel the multiple pieces of my truth in this season than to look inside my purse, both literally and metaphorically.

A woman's purse is not just for looks and head turns, but it carries some of her most treasured belongings. She not only keeps it close to her to guard it from unwanted violators, but will only entrust it to a few familiar friends or family members to hold it until she returns. Which speaks more about the sacredness of what we carry inside than the label that is adorned on the outside.

There's bound to be trails of my truth found in the various pockets of my purse. So, before we begin the plunge into the contents of my sassy satchel, I thought I'd first share with you what it might sound like if it could ACTUALLY talk. I'm sure it would have a whole lot to say! Let's listen.

"Girl, seriously...did you forget about me and the hidden treasures that I have deep inside of me? Well, from where I'm sitting, it sure does feel that way!

I used to be you're go-to bag...your ride or die carry all. I was the first (real) fashion labeled bag you rocked. I was your sassy satchel! Wherever you went, there I was holding all of your treasures without complaint! I made you feel bold and full of life when you walked with me into any room! Now, look at me. I'm tattered, torn and thrown on the floor. Wow! How did I get here? And why have I been here for so long? And look at YOU trying to make appearances without me securely attached to your shoulder. It just doesn't seem to work. You're just not yourself.

I never thought I'd see the day that we would part ways. What did I do to make you forget about me and all of the phenomenal pieces of treasure I contain? What's sad, is that you don't even realize that you left so much behind in me. I'm carrying beloved pieces that have yet to be revealed and have never seen the light of day. Did you forget about these?

Sure, you've looked for me a time or two, but when it was apparent that it was going to take a lot more effort to find me and the treasures you thought you lost, you abandoned your search.

Well, I've been here patiently waiting to make a reappearance, but you stiiiiiillll haven't searched hard enough to find me. But, I'm still here...in the back of the closet...on the floor...under your pile of fabulous shoes...waiting on you to discover me again. Search harder for me, dig deeper and be courageous enough to pull me out and put me back in my rightful position with all the treasures I have inside of me waiting to be rediscovered. We have a lot more to do and you need all of these amazing treasures to do it!"

Hidden Treasure

Have you ever carried your purse for so long that it developed a gaping hole in the bottom of the inner lining? Guilty! Girl, don't act like you don't know what I'm talking about (well, if you don't carry a purse, you might not). I know I'm not the only one that's had something sharp penetrate the inner lining of a purse and cause this type of heartbreaking damage.

In fact, the purse you're carrying right now just might be in this condition. If that's you, no judgement here, girl!

I've really never been the one to collect multiple styles of purses. It just wasn't my thing. When I was younger, my mother had a hard enough time getting me to wear a pair of pumps and a dress, let alone carry a purse. Fast forward to today, I love a fabulous pair of heels and I've treated myself to some really nice purses. However, I'm still not quite the fabulous diva that changes her purse with every outfit or with every season for that matter. I find a really cute, sturdy purse and I rock her until I'm pretty much forced to change her or the mood strikes me to rotate her. So admittedly, the tragedy of the gaping hole has happened to me on a few occasions.

One of my favorite purses developed a gaping hole in the bottom lining that was the size of an orange. So, I was forced to grab a new purse and transfer the contents, of my now damaged purse, to the new one. My new purse was cute, but it took some getting used to. I didn't quite feel myself without my favorite bag, but there was nothing I could do at this point, the damage was already done. So, I moved forward and made the new purse a part of my journey for the season.

As I was out and about one Saturday, doing what I do, I had the urge to reapply my lip gloss. So, I reached into my bag to find the sparkly lip gloss that made my lips pop and my beautiful butterfly mirror to ensure I put it on just right. I found the lip gloss, but I was still blindly feeling around for my mirror. I dumped the purse out and rummaged through the contents, only to discover it wasn't there amongst all my other treasures. I was so disappointed because that mirror meant a lot to me. The compact mirror was silver with a beautiful diamond butterfly that sat on the very top. I purchased it to remind myself that I was uncaged and free to fly in my purpose; so you can imagine how upset I was when I couldn't find it. All I could think about was, *where and when did I lose it* and *why did it take me so long to notice it was missing.* I searched high and low for that mirror and sadly couldn't find it anywhere.

Several months went by and I went on carrying my new purse, but I still felt some kind of way about my missing treasured mirror. I didn't make an effort to replace it because I truly wouldn't have felt the same about it.

Discovered Treasure

Are you a spring cleaner? It's not my favorite thing to do, but it's so rewarding when I'm finished. I clean out my pantry, my dresser and my closets to free up space! Well, during one of my cleaning frenzies, I was cleaning out my closet and I found my sassy satchel! My treasured purse, my first fashion labeled carry all was in the back of the closet on the floor. I picked it up, dusted it off and began examining the left over contents in it and was quickly reminded of the gaping hole in its inner lining. As my hand made its way to the inside of the hole, I discovered several items had fallen down into it so I began taking them out one by one. To my surprise, I felt something familiar and excitedly pulled out my beautiful butterfly mirror! It had fallen into that gaping hole and had been there all this time covered with wrappers and residue. It wasn't lost, it was just hidden!

The past few years have been such an incredible ride. I made some hard decisions and faced some tough challenges as it pertained to the brokenness of my past. Hurtful life trials caused me to forget my worth and value. But with God, I fought hard to rebuild myself. Because of that healing work, I'm now able to say that I'm a survivor of the violence I experienced at the hands of my sister's abuser. I can now openly receive the love that God has for me and the calling He placed on my life. I'm boldly using my gifts and talents to bring glory to His name and helping other women do the same. I guess you can say I got my S.W.A.G. Back! But, (yes, there's a "but" coming) after some deep self-reflection at the beginning of 2018, I realized that although I was definitely not in the emotional dark place I used to be in, I still felt like there was something weighing heavily on me. . Huh? How could this be? I thought I was free.

Upon further reflection, I was brought to the conclusion that, like my treasured butterfly mirror, there were still pieces of me tucked away in a gaping hole. "Why was I still hiding?" , was the question I kept asking myself after coming to this profound realization.

This wasn't the first time I felt this way, but it had been a long time since I confronted myself in this manner. I thought I'd done all the necessary work to unmask myself and live authentically. So, why did I feel like parts of me were still in hiding and why did it take me so long to notice? The honest answer is that I did notice, but I wasn't sure or prepared to truly deal with it. And just like that, the mask that I so desperately worked hard to remove, reappeared. I found myself hiding my true thoughts, feelings and desires because it was much easier than saying what I really wanted or needed. I was giving into the fear that kept me from moving into the next level of my life, so I assumed I had reached my peak. Wow! Here I was again. I knew it was time for me to do something different, if I wanted something different. Instead of keeping this realization to myself, as I've been known to do in the past, I shared it with the person that helps me keep my inner lining in tact – my sister and wonder twin, FaLisa.

Revelation from My Inner Lining

BOOM! That's how hard it hit me when my sister shared a message that God laid on her heart pertaining to me.

His message to me was: *"You are no longer caged; you've been released. You are choosing to stay on familiar ground and it's time to launch into the deep and cast your net wider. I've protected you this far. I'm pleased with you, but don't take steps backwards for anyone. You have conditioned yourself for the valleys and it's time for mountain tops."*

So, there it was...my truth...unfolded right in front of me. Needless to say, I was in awe. Through my sister, the Lord confirmed that I was CHOOSING to stay hidden and allowing fear to talk me out of my future.

I had convinced myself it was easier to keep parts of me hidden rather than expose the fullness of what God created in me. I had been playing it safe; preventing myself from moving towards greater things that would challenge the comfortable setting of my life. I had allowed other people's insecurities and negative comments to define my limits and stop me from pursuing all that God had for me. Somewhere along the way I was sold on the idea that I'd done enough already and I would lose everything I loved if I pursued more. Fear challenged my faith and I became comfortable with hiding in that hole.

The enemy tried to use discouragement and fear to disrupt the dream that God has for me. He was hoping that I would give up and stay hidden in that gaping hole; lost, afraid and exhausted from trying to climb out. He was hoping that I wouldn't realize that God still had plans to use me and that He had something miraculous planned for me. It was a hard reality to accept, but I was so grateful for the revelation.

You may have found your way into a gaping hole; tucked away, quietly hiding your magnificence from the world. It takes wisdom to recognize it and courage to fight your way out of it. I've had countless conversations with women who've hidden their treasured gifts because they didn't recognize their worth or were too afraid to communicate it to the world. Our unwillingness to see and speak about our value, keeps us hidden and puts us in a position to be undervalued and taken for granted. Consequently, we accept what others think we're worth verses what we're ACTUALLY worth.

Because of fear and self-limiting beliefs, many of us aren't living up to our full potential. We aren't using our voices to ask for what we want or need. So, as a result, we miss out on some of the greatest opportunities in both our personal and professional lives. You, my gorgeous sister, have beautiful treasures inside of you waiting to be discovered, waiting to be set free. So, I ask you to reflect on these 4 questions:

1. What's inside of you that needs to be revealed?
2. What value do you bring?
3. What's holding you back?
4. Is it time for you to dig deep and uncover your hidden treasures?

We are reminded several times through scripture that we are not to BE afraid or discouraged because God is with us (Joshua 1:9). He didn't say that we would never FEEL fear, we're still human; but we do have to face it. That's where courage comes in.

It begins with the conversations that you have with yourself. What are you telling yourself you can't do or you're not worthy of? The "aha" moment here is that nobody can talk you into or out of YOUR destiny. As fabulous as my circle of friends and family are, they can't talk me into my destiny. No, that's my job. I had to change the way I thought about and spoke to myself so that I could come out of hiding. I was the one responsible for talking myself into my destiny. *What are you talking yourself out of that God is trying to push you into?*

Fear was limiting me from fully pursuing the thing God was calling me toward. Fear had me believe that if I moved in that direction it would cost me something. I wasn't sure how, but

I was certain I would lose things I held precious in my life. The truth is, yes, moving toward what God has for me may cost me something...time, resources, effort, comfort, but the outcome is far greater than the cost and definitely worth the pursuit. I still have more treasures in me to be used and it was time for me to be courageous enough to take the limits off.

I guess you're probably wondering what happened to my sassy satchel with that gaping hole! Well, I decided to keep her as a reminder to keep my treasures from being hidden (plus she's really cute and nothing a little sewing kit can't fix!). There's a lot more inside of me waiting to be revealed...waiting to be set free! The Lord didn't give me gifts and talents to hurt me or for me to hide them. No, He trusted me to use them to impact the lives of others. I'm a firm believer that when I'm fully living in my purpose, I help someone else live in their's. What a sad situation it would've been had I not reached this conclusion, because hiding in that gaping hole almost prevented me from launching and publishing _"If Her Purse Could Talk"_.

I've decided that I'm no longer hiding my treasures. Instead, I'm giving myself permission to courageously explore my inner lining and pull them all out. I'm no longer accepting how others define me, but instead I'm helping them redefine their definition of me. I'm consistently challenging myself to move out of my Comfort Zone to boldly walking in my

Courage Zone where I can see the mountain tops that God has for me.

I confidently declare I am DISCOVERED treasure, no longer hidden!

Purse Prayer:

Heavenly Father,

You are so magnificent in all of Your ways. Thank You for allowing me to rediscover the treasures You placed inside of me. Your Word reminds me that You did not place in me a spirit of fear, but of power and a sound mind, so it's ok for me to come out of hiding. Help me to be courageous enough to take the limits off that others have tried to place on me. Silence the noise of my own insecurities. Please help me thoughtfully use my gifts and talents to impact the world and bring glory to Your name. I pray that the woman reading this will find the courage to open her purse, climb out of her gaping hole and rediscover the true worth and value of her treasures.

In Your Precious Name, Amen.

DeYonne Parker

DeYonne Parker, Nebraska Corn Husker turned Georgia Peach, is the published author of the "life-changing" book and curriculum, *"Girl, Get Your S.W.A.G. Back!"* and the Visionary, Compiler and Lead Author of *"If Her Purse Could Talk"*.

Parker's greatest joy in life is being the loving wife and mother to her handsome husband and 2 amazing sons, who she affectionately calls her Mr. Parkers.

In addition, DeYonne is a multi-national, professional speaker, facilitator, author and empowerment coach. Her mission is to empower ladies and leaders to be what and who they were called to be. She has spent over 20 years of her life pouring into the lives of others to help them rebuild, regain and reclaim the life they truly desire and deserve to live.

Parker has been blessed to grace stages and corporate classrooms around the world. From Kenya, South Africa, Canada, China, Argentina, UAE, Belgium to various states in the U.S. , DeYonne motivates the masses with her powerful and riveting messages.

Parker is also the Founder of The S.W.A.G. University and Vice President of Gem Makers, LLC. where she and her team empower ladies and leaders to get their S.W.A.G. back and walk in their full potential.

99

1 Am...

Discovered treasure
No longer hidden by my own doubts and fears.
God has shined His glorious light on me

~ DeYonne Parker ~

Chapter 8

Let Go, Let God and Stay in Your Lane!
By J.S. Littleton

Like most people, I've been asked all kinds of questions during my lifetime, but nothing like, "If your purse could talk, what would it say?" I initially thought, "What a provocative question?" This may sound strange, but days later it seemed as if I was on an imaginary highway.

That unusual question provoked me to travel down Memory Lane to places and seasons in my life I had locked away; but in order to answer the question, I had to take that trip back. Ready or not, I took a deep breath, buckled my mental seatbelt, and asked God to protect my heart and mind during this journey.

It seemed as if I there were signs directing me to where I had to go to find the answer. Signs like, "Deeper", "Open your eyes!", "Go deeper", "Don't cry", "You're almost there", "Don't be afraid", and finally, "Welcome home, it is here you will find the answer to, *If your purse could talk, what would she say?*"

Finally, I reached my destination and envisioned myself

standing before my childhood home with a note on the door which read, "Your story begins inside. There you will find the answers you have been searching for all your life, so tell your story without sanitizing it and without being superficial, and lock the door when you leave!"

Laying The Foundation For My "Stuff"

From the time I was born until the time I left home after graduating from high school, the foundation for my "stuff" began inside my home; the one place which should have been a safe haven. From the time I was able to comprehend the difference between love and kindness vs. that of anger and physical pain, I began to "stuff" things inside because as a child I could not process the contradictions, dysfunction, and insanity in the place I called home.

While my physical body was safe until age 6 or 7, throughout my childhood I have vivid memories of the physical and emotional violence my mom endured at the hands of my dad. He was 23 years older than her and they were married 20 years before he died.

My mother left the comfort and support of her family down south and moved to start life anew with my dad in West Virginia; a coal miner who worked hard to provide for his family. Looking back in retrospect, I often wonder what deep, dark things my father encountered having been born in the year 1900 in the south that would fill him with such anger and rage. His large, muscular body didn't compare to mom's tall, thin frame, and although he never abused me, he beat her religiously on weekends and holidays unless we were on vacation or had guests.

Many decades later in 2001, my mother and I talked openly about her life with my dad and she told me the beatings began a few hours after they were married, and went on for almost 19 years. The reason he didn't beat her the last year of his life was because of me and I found that to be ironic as I learned more about this woman who loved God and who tried to teach me what it meant to love Him with all your heart. Eventually I got it and years before she died, we experienced many, many years together talking about the God who loves us and I thank God for those special memories.

According to her, when I was 2 mom was tired of being beaten, kicked, and told to get out of HIS house. She said he was the first and only person to call her names or to deliberately hurt her; basically opening her eyes to the ugly side of life! It took strength for her to pack her Samsonite suitcase and carry me as she walked to the bus stop on a cold, snowy day. Unfortunately my dad found us before the bus came and I reached for him to pick me up as most children would do. Without apologizing or saying a word to my mom, he took me in his arms and began walking home; leaving her standing alone on the side of the road in the snow. Hearing her recall this story saddened me because I knew the price she paid for the decision she made that day. She made a decision to stay in an abusive situation for her child's sake because she grew up without a father and didn't want to repeat that pattern.

I found it unimaginable that for almost 19 years she allowed herself to be treated worse than the dogs we had just because my 2 year old self wanted my dad to pick me up. However, I am forever grateful for those conversations because ironically. I learned that from the time I was 3 years old, I made numerous attempts to physically protect her.

As years past and eventually my dad retired, he increased his violent, drunken rants from only weekends and holidays to whenever he wanted to, but being a teenager at that time, I had witnessed enough! One morning as he was beating mom something in me snapped and before I knew it, I grabbed one of his sharp, pointed weapons and once again jumped to the defense of my mom; striking him repeatedly from behind because I didn't want to accidently hit her in the process.

When the weapon I was using got caught in the threads of his powder blue sweater and his blood began to spread, I snapped out of it as he began turning my way. When he looked at me, I did what I always did, I took off running as fast as I could to a family member's house. Hours later mom came looking for me and told me I only drew blood but my dad was okay. I think I cried from frustration thinking to myself, how long will this go on?

By "drawing blood", I got his attention and he too came looking for me because he had something to say. He told me to get in the car and in a soft voice he said, "I love you more than life itself, but if you ever hit me again I WILL KILL YOU!" I was no longer afraid, but I was shocked because I had **NEVER** heard him say the word, "love" before. I couldn't speak so I just stared at him, knowing in my heart that if he EVER laid hands on my mom in a violent way again, I was willing to die trying to protect her.

He never hit her again, and I often wondered if the strain of NOT hitting her, along with health issues, lead to his death a year later. I like to believe he loved me enough to not place us in jeopardy of killing one another. For the first time in my life, I finally knew mom was physically safe even though she was forever scarred by the man who promised to love her.

My journey down Memory Lane helped me to see the how and why of my story by showing me how a foundation was laid which caused a sad little girl to "stuff" those things she didn't understand deep within the depths of her soul.

The Death Of Innocence

When I was a child I carried a "pocketbook". It was cute, small, and carried on Sundays and special occasions. It held a pair of gloves with lace along the top to match the lace around my socks, several pieces of peppermint candy, a tiny handmade handkerchief given to me by my mom, and money for the offering plate at church. For many years I enjoyed dressing up and carrying my little "pocketbook" because I got compliments. By the time I was 7 or 8, I no longer wanted anyone to compliment me on anything I wore, especially men!

During my childhood I sustained emotional, psychological, mental, and spiritual harm at home, but it wasn't until I was 7 or 8 years old that I would encounter physical harm. Not at the hands of my father, but at the hands of an evil, wicked child molester in our community who would forever change the lives of me and my best friend.

Recruited by a young neighbor, and lured by the monster of a man, my best friend and I were sexually violated and told we could "never" tell anyone, our parents wouldn't love us anymore if they knew; people would think we were "nasty lil' girls", and the biggest lie of all was that he wouldn't hurt us!

Over and over our innocence was shattered into so many

pieces it could never be repaired or replaced. As young, defenseless, vulnerable children we believed ALL the lies, never knowing that every detail would be seared into our minds like cows being branded.

During that time, I knew I was changing because my mom asked questions but I didn't trust myself to answer or share the truth without crying. It was eating me up that my mom was worried about me when she had enough pain in her life. That gave me the courage to fight the last time he put his hands on me and I screamed, "I'm going to tell my dad!" which allowed both me and my friend to escape and run to safety.

We were incapable of thoroughly understanding the full impact of how those countless days in hell would alter our concept of who we were; what we thought of ourselves; and whether we could or would ever be able to trust again. All that and more would change the essence of who we were before losing our innocence.

When my dad heard my story, he didn't tell me he loved me, but he showed me by how tightly he held me and by the tears I saw in his eyes as he went into the house to get his gun. He then walked out in search of the abuser to bring justice for his child.

We later learned that my friend and I weren't the only ones who ran. My dad had a reputation that proceeded him, and needless to say, the abuser knew he'd better be gone when my dad came for him.

In spite of the bad memories, that day I realized my dad loved me enough to kill if someone hurt me. Little did I know that one day many years later he would actually say the words "I love you", but sadly it was in response to my attempt to kill him when I was a teen. That was the season the foundation for my "stuff" was completed and firmly laid by two men who had "stuff" of their own.

One Messed Up Kid

For 19 years I lived with domestic violence in my home and was the victim of sexual molestation by someone in the community. In a twisted way, because my dad wasn't able to avenge my abuser, he became obsessed with preparing me to protect myself. He was extremely overprotective to the point of waiving his gun at times if he saw a boy walking toward our steps. He routinely put me through a series of "What if . . ." scenarios and by the time I was 15 he had developed a "List of Rules to Live By", all designed to make me "feel" strong, confident, and capable of standing my ground when needed.

Honestly, I was one messed up kid as I observed him teaching me, his daughter, to be strong and self-sufficient while beating my mom unmercifully when she attempted to exhibit the same attributes. It messed me up knowing my dad valued and protected me more than he did my mom, but I knew my mom wanted the same things for me so I listened and I learned.

My mom lived a life that was pleasing to God even though she admitted that once she cried out to Him when one of my dad's brutal beatings put her in the hospital. It was the only time she recalled asking God what she had done to be treated the way she was being treated. She didn't "hear" God's answer, but she promised herself that night that she would NEVER cry again and sadly I think she kept that promise.

As for my dad, I don't know how he felt about God or himself. I know he never tried to stop us from going to church but he also never had a nice thing to say about anyone in the church, including my mom. There was no mention of God in anything he taught me. His focus was on being strong, independent, self-sufficient, never letting a man hit me and never running from a fight.

Good Times And Some Not So Good

After leaving my hometown and moving to Washington D.C., I found myself in love. Damaged though I may have been, within 17 months I was entering into a new season by marrying my first boyfriend and becoming a teenage bride.

For the first 2-3 years of our marriage things were slim and money was tight so a small purse fit my preference and it met my needs. However 3 years later I needed a larger purse and a diaper bag.

As a young wife and a new mother I was learning things I never thought I'd have to know. After all, getting married and having a child were NEVER on my radar. For one thing, I had never seen a healthy marriage and as for having a baby, my doctor said I wouldn't be able to conceive or carry a child . . . But God had other plans! Mom was there for the first two weeks after the baby arrived; all I had to do was nurse her. When she left, I cried for days thinking about all the things I didn't know . . . But God!

In spite of all that, I was lucky, I had a loving husband who did everything he could to help before and after I gave birth (but was a Nervous Nelly during my pregnancy). We still didn't have much money, but we had a lot of love and I thought we had an awesome "family". What happened? Where did that funky season come from after the 12th or 13th year of marriage when we were close to becoming a "broken" family?

At some point, the atmosphere began to change in our home and invisible brick after brick was thrown into the mix. The first was that of mental distance; then came one of silence, with both of us locking up all those unspoken words; then the brick of emotional distance, and ladies, I'm sure you already know that the final brick was that of physical distance.

New Beginnings

There came a point when, I knew I NO LONGER WANTED TO BE MARRIED . . . and I stepped into a brand new, multi-faceted season as a "single mom". Interestingly enough, I was less afraid of being a single mom than I was when our daughter was born; and I still carried a big purse at times.

Our daughter was in elementary school, my financial resources were jacked up, my mom was disappointed (remember, she was a "til death do us part" kindda girl), and 99% of "our" married friends would no longer take my calls (not even the wives).

In spite of all that, I was determined to be strong for my daughter, to never put my "stuff" on her, and to make sure that she always came first and didn't want for anything within reason. After all, she didn't ask for her world to be turned upside down. Why should she suffer because her parents had lost their minds and didn't know how to communicate or compromise?

Being a single mom was very challenging for lots of reasons, but the entire process helped make me a better mom because we had more one-on-one time; that is until she went into that "weird" place known only to teens. However caring for our daughter gave me no time to deal with my "stuff".

Caution: Heavy Load

Once our daughter went off to college, I failed to use that time to slow down. Instead I was spending even more time with work, politics, networking, and a host of other things. In the process of doing those things, I was still helping others when needed. Eventually, the "stuff" I carried for other people, personally and professionally, began to weigh me down when added to my own. It was time for me to deal with my life.

In hindsight, I was better off having the innocence of a child and carrying a little girl's "pocketbook" that only held a pair of gloves, candy, a handkerchief, and money for the church offering plate.

All I Need Is A Little More Jesus

I always believed my reason for being on the planet was to meet the needs of others and I always tried to help when needed, but it never dawned on me to call on God because of my childhood impressions of Him and because I had been taught to be strong and self-sufficient.

There were times when I "felt" as if God was trying to get my attention, but to no avail. But in June 1999 the unexpected death of my brother threw me in a downward spiral but a visitation of his spirit gave me the strength to gradually pull away from pouring everything I had into others while ignoring myself. God saw my broken heart and felt my anger and pain, and saw the shadow of a dark spirit of deep sadness sucking the life from my body. For the first time, I realized I wasn't in control and God had my attention.

God loves me so much that He "brought" my brother's spirit into my bedroom a week before Thanksgiving in 1999. Even in my deepest sadness, I recognized my brother's voice call my name and there was no fear or doubt in my mind that it was his spirit I felt close to me. He spoke softly like our mom and he began to counsel me by telling me not to be sad, but to surround myself with positive people and to always have a grateful heart. When he "left", he left a little part of his spirit with me because my tears dried up and I was able to smile and celebrate Thanksgiving with my family.

After my brother's death in 1999, I wasted 2 years chasing other religions and looking for anything that might help me purge myself of my "stuff" and to gain inner peace.

Each time I shared my adventures with my daughter, she **screamed**, "Jesus, mom, you need Jesus. Stop this foolishness!" Too bad I didn't listen to her the first time. But God was patient and He waited for that set time when I was willing to surrender to His will for my life because I finally realized I wasn't as strong as I thought!

But I finally turned to Him and He re-ordered my way of thinking and on November 2, 2001, I finally got out of my own way so that I could give myself and ALL my "stuff" to who could handle it. The God who created me and put a dream in my heart

Surrendering my will to God has been the best decision of my life and the most interesting journey thus far. Regardless of what's going on around me or in my body, I wake up each morning anticipating what God will reveal throughout the day. He has surrounded me with Godly people who lovingly lift me up when darkness tries to slip up on me and I am truly blessed that He never gave up on me.

"Let Go, Let God, And Stay In Your Lane!"

My God is awesome and meets ALL my needs and I receive a bonus every time He smiles down on me or makes me laugh. He speaks to me in my language and when I hear, "What are you doing?" I imagine His head leaning as He looks at me and I crack up because I still have those days when I "temporarily" lose my mind and I laugh because He's reminding me to stay in my lane!

By looking in the rearview mirror of life, I think my purse is ready to answer the question, *"If your purse could talk, what would it say?".* You can't see me, but I'm smiling right now because my purse would say: *"**Let go, let God and stay in your lane!**"*

Yep, that's what she would say. Nowadays my purse is small and cannot hold much at all . . . just like me! Sure, I continue to help and bless others when led, but not before seeking God as I try to stay in my lane!

Finding Peace At Last

This journey has been painful and exhausting, and that's probably why it took me so long to deal with my "stuff". As I struggled with deciding how much of my "stuff" to share, I can say without a doubt that this process was almost as intense as the original situations which actually left their marks on my heart, mind, body, and spirit so many years ago.

Things so painful I had to stuff them somewhere because, even as a kid, I always knew I wasn't equipped mentally, physically, emotionally, or spiritually to adequately handle the "stuff" I faced as a child.

I have always wanted to know and understand why I am wired the way I am and going back in time helped me to understand things I had forgotten while revealing things I never knew because I didn't understand the importance of history and timing.

I hope you enjoyed reading my story and allowing me to unpack my purse, because as difficult as it was, my load is now much lighter. I've honestly enjoyed sharing the revelations I received while going back in time. Because of you, I went deeper than I ever imagined . . . But God was with me all the way and carried me through the darkest parts of my past while drying my tears during the saddest parts. Take care, and remember that you are NEVER alone even when you think you are.

Purse Prayer:

God, I thank You for allowing me to be among those chosen to participate in this project. Thank You for holding my hand with every step we took as we stopped along the way in our walk down Memory Lane. Thank You for the healing of past hurts which have kept me bound for much too long and I thank You for drying ALL my tears from the beginning of this journey to putting the last period to end my story. I pray that You will use the testimonies of each contributor to open the eyes, minds, and hearts of each and every person who will hold a copy of this book in their hands and that it will be a blessing to them. I pray all these things Father, in the Mighty Name of Jesus.

Amen.

J.S. Littleton

J. S. Littleton is a retiree who has accomplished many things and received many achievements and recognition during the course of her life. She is incredibly thankful for all the shoulders she stood on and for those who mentored her throughout her many endeavors. However, her greatest joy is her daughter Nicole Steele who has blessed her with a wonderful son-in-law, Rick, and two beautiful granddaughters, Jadyn and Victoria.

Littleton deeply believes the best decision she ever made was to re-dedicate her life to Christ November 2, 2001, and since then, she has been experiencing unspeakable joy in finally knowing who and whose she is and who she was created to be at this stage of her life.

Chapter 9

Counterfeit Carryall to Classic Coach

By Dr. Nicole Steele

I haven't always had an appreciation for quality purses and handbags. That has been something that I have come to develop over the years.

It might have something to do with my past. I can distinctly recall growing up as a teen in the early 80's when the trend of gold bamboo earrings, custom name plates and Gucci and Louis Vuitton handbags were the big thing. There were a lot of things vying for the attention of an insecure and impressionable teen girl. It may have been the influence of artist like Salt-N- Pepper or the words of LL Cool J with songs like "Around the Way Girl" ringing in my head.

All I know is that where I came from, name brands had weight. Maybe it was a Michigan thing or maybe it was just a perception being developed in my young mind.

While I believed the hype and bought into the pressures of fitting the image and looking the part projected by the media and others, the one person who hadn't bought into it was my momma.

I recall begging her for certain designer wear and handbags, but she was not moved. As a single parent, putting me in designer things to impress people I wouldn't even remember a few years down the line wasn't on her list of priorities at all.

Don't get me wrong, my mother was a true fashionista. Not only did she dress in style, but she LOVED shopping. In fact, she describes herself as having a "black belt" in shopping. She could find deals out of this world and would actually plan our vacations around which shopping malls were in close proximity. Despite that fact, she still wasn't moved by me begging and pleading for expensive designer handbags.

I recall my friends telling me about the knock-off, bootleg bags which could be found at the local flea market, and that became my focus. Maybe, just maybe, I could get a knock-off bag that "looked real". Who cared if the stitching was off, the designer logo was flawed or the quality of leather wasn't quite right? Who was I going to allow to get that close anyway?

For me it wasn't about quality at all, instead it was all about appearance and image. My drive for approval was more important and kept me obsessed with looking the part, even if I knew deep within that I was perpetrating the fraud.

I was unaware that the counterfeit carryall purses I had become obsessed with had actually become an analogy of my reality. There I was living a lie. The habits of trying to impress others and this twisted way of thinking was becoming a regular routine which subsequently carried into my young adult years.

As I went off to college, I was living my life as a counterfeit on some levels. I was allowing the opinion and expectations of others to be stuffed into my mind and spirit for me to carry and attempt to live up to. Me, and my bootleg bags were on the edge, and I was trying hard to keep it all together.

It had become the norm, so much so, that even I didn't realize that I had an issue. Looking the part, fitting the mold, and trying to measure up became my method of operation. I learned to master it pretty well and even began to believe the lie for myself.

It's not that those closest to me were placing pressures on me to be what I really wasn't. It was more self-imposed pressure I was placing upon myself.

Get Your Purse Off The Ground

The thing with counterfeit, low quality merchandise is the same as counterfeit and low quality living. When it comes to counterfeit purses for instance, you don't mind who handles them or where you place them. You will set them down anywhere, allow them to be exposed to any kind of conditions and allow others to carry them or stuff their things in them.

I remember when I was growing up, my grandmother would always instruct me to never place her purse on the floor. It didn't matter if the carpet was recently vacuumed or floor mopped. Folklore had been passed down for generations that if you allowed your purse to be on the ground you would be broke.

I think about my grandmothers "pocketbook", as she called it, and all the wonderful things she would stuff in it. From her bright pink lipstick, to her handy dandy coin purse, to the Starlight mints she would give me to keep quiet when she took me to church. No matter the day, there were things I was sure to find in her purse if needed.

When I think about my counterfeit carryall, it was a different story. The items I would carry varied. A few had value but most didn't. I would throw in whatever I needed to fill it up. Ironically, the same was true in my spirit. There was a void within that I didn't realize until much later in life. I was subconsciously attempting to fill the void I had within with the affirmation and approval of others. There I was stuffing unnecessary things in my physical purse while at the same time allowing others to stuff unwanted things into my emotional and spiritual purse.

Girl, Put That Bag Down

Did I look the part and fit the mold? Most definitely. Was I exhausted from the self-imposed pressure I was under? No doubt. I looked the part but had no clue of who I was or where I was going.

If my purse could talk at that time in my life, I am sure it would have said something like, *"Child, don't you see me struggling? I'm busting at the seams here while you appear to be clueless. What are you thinking? Can you please take some of this unnecessary weight off me? Please take this mess out of here and lighten this load! Hey lady, I was not made for this!"*

In reality, not only was my purse not made for that life, neither was I! Up until that point, I had been allowing my value and worth to be determined by external things and other people. I was living life on the surface but unwilling or perhaps unable to go deep.

Maybe it was the "daddy issues" I carried deep within but hadn't yet come to address head-on. Or perhaps my carryall was being filled with the sweet nothings of guys being used to fill an empty void. Or maybe, just maybe, my insecurities came from my secret fear of success.

Yes, that's right. Could it be that I wasn't dealing with the fear of failure that many wrestle with, but instead was subconsciously dealing with the fear of success? Perhaps deep within I knew what I was really made of, but just wasn't ready or willing to pay the cost to do the work needed to make it a reality. Maybe my desire to please others was more appealing although it kept me in a box, trapped and bound.

My desire for the approval of others trumped my desire to be all I was created to be. Just maybe I allowed the insecurities of others and their inability to handle all the greatness packed within me to place unimaginable limits on myself. I know I am not alone, so don't judge me.

In fact over the years I have met countless women and girls who have found themselves trapped and bound in similar ways. What is it about us? We often do such a great job at affirming and building up others, but when it comes to doing the same for ourselves, we don't have a clue. Eventually I learn the hard way that when it comes to counterfeit merchandise and counterfeit living, you get what you pay for.

I finally realized that there had to be more to life than simply going through the motions and getting the same results. In reality I needed to own up to my counterfeit carryall living and begin to lighten my load by tossing out some bad habits, negative thoughts and unhealthy associations. The big question I had to ask myself is if I was willing to pay the cost?

Are You Willing To Pay The Price?

There came a point where I didn't have to rely on my mother to buy a designer hand bag for me.

I started working at age 14 and started making money that could have easily been put aside for a nice bag or designer tote, but if the truth be told, I wasn't willing to pay the price. The thought of the countless hours of hard work needed to buy something so expensive was unimaginable. You see it was much easier to focus on the superficial opposed to substance.

Well, I'm glad to say that trouble don't last always. At some point along the journey the haze and fog was removed from my eyes and I was introduced to the Truth. For the first time in my life, I had a close encounter with a God who gave me clarity about how He saw me. Not only did I learn that He loved me unconditionally with all my flaws and faults, I learned that I am an original design, custom created with a divine destiny. It was during that pivotal time that I came into a true understanding of WHO and WHOSE I was.

I was astonished to learn that God created and knit me together in my mother's womb. I learned that He placed unique gifts, talents, and abilities deep within me, as He has done for you.

I learned that the only opinion of me that matters is His and slowly but surely I began to shift my thinking. As I began to shift my thinking, everything else began to follow.

I wish I could say it was easy breezy, but I'd be lying. There was a lot of work I had to do to reframe my thoughts and deal with my own insecurities and the things that had me bound and stuck for so long. I not only had to do the work, but I had to be willing to count the cost.

Doors had to be closed to some relationships and some friendships along the way as I came to understand-that not everyone was going where I was going. It's not that others don't have a choice to progress forward, but some just aren't interested or willing to do the work and make the investment.

As a result I had to endure many seasons of loneliness which were downright difficult; especially for someone who relied so heavily on the approval of others. It cost me seasons of isolation as God began to reconstruct my heart and mind, but I made it through.

It cost me going to some painful places emotionally and having to face myself, my past failures and my personal flaws. It wasn't always pretty and it required me to acknowledge some things that for a long time I was unaware of or unwilling to face head on.

This journey of self-discovery has also cost me financially. It cost me the comfort and security of a corporate career that was once an obsession. I had to be willing to shed the image of success I had formed, in exchange for an active pursuit of my purpose and God's plan for my life.

It was during these crucial times that I have come to know the faithfulness of God. In retrospect, those moments have become some of the sweetest because I have learned how to love myself the way God loves me. I allowed His plans and vision for my life to be fused with my own as I began to see Him connect all the dots of my past into a glorious picture of my future. I learned to trust Him and Him alone and have seen Him do what only He can do.

He has helped me break habits and helped me shift my mindset. He has poured into me when I have been at my lowest points and shown me things about myself that amaze me. Through it all, He has shown me that I am built for greatness, and guess what...so are you!

Upgrade

As I got older and moved into adulthood, my tastes began to change. When it came to my accessories, I was encouraged to invest in some staple items, one being a good black purse. That's around the time that I was introduced and fell in love with Coach bags. Though Coach had their trendy lines of handbags, they always kept a constant stock of their classic designs. Though the prices exceeded more than I was used to paying for purses and handbags, the quality and craftsmanship was unmatched. What do you know? The time had come for me to trade in my counterfeit carryall for a classic Coach.

It's funny how things change. When it came to my first Coach bag, I took great care of it. I was selective in when I carried it and very particular about where I placed it. I was very careful not to scuff or scrape it, and I dared somebody to ask me to borrow it. To say the least, I was protecting my investment.

I began to take on the same mindset personally. I began to make the investment in myself and to protect my heart and mind in ways I hadn't before. You see, once I became clear of WHO I was and WHOSE I was, God began to make clear my WHY and WHAT. Why was I created and what I was created to do became my focus. I realized that I had been chasing the wrong things and my pursuit of success was inaccurate. Up until that point, success for me meant climbing the corporate ladder, and obtaining a cushy office in a big city high rise. I had big dreams and big plans and nothing and no one was going to stop me from achieving those dreams.

That was until God snatched my counterfeit purse, threw it out of the window and took the wheel in my life. I later learned that while success was great and I had made great strides as I charted my course in that direction, significance was what God had in mind. He actually wanted me to use those painful and embarrassing seasons of my past to help others.

What??? You mean God wanted me to be willing to share details on the personal insecurities of my past that I was finally coming to grips with? He wanted me to put myself on blast and openly share with others the years I had lived a lie and foolishly made decisions and allowed others to dictate my destiny. How in the world could that level of transparency and out right embarrassment, be beneficial and guide me towards a life of significance?

Now it's funny, not only had God allowed me to trade in my counterfeit carryall purses for the real deal, but He was trading in my vision and re-charting my destiny. He took me from Corporate Climber to that of Confidence Coach. He was actually taking all those painful and embarrassing things in my past and working them out together for His good.

In fact it has been those things specifically that have allowed me to impact the lives of so many women and girls over the years. From the formation of Diamond In The Rough Youth Development Program which strives to empower girls and prevent them from making similar mistakes; to the development of Gem Makers, LLC which empowers women both personally and professionally. I had no earthly idea that the pain and price of my past could actually be used for a significant purpose.

A New *"PURSEpective"*

I remember the day over a decade ago, my sister and mother suggested that I make pink my signature color and make it a habit to wear something PINK everyday as a reminder of my life's purpose which is to **P**repare, **I**nspire, **N**urture and provide **K**nowledge to others.

I remember actually being offended and totally dismissing the thought as I screamed, "I'm not doing that!" It's funny how words taste as you eat them. Despite my apprehension, I subconsciously took their advice, and with the help of my mother (the same one who never lost her skills or love for shopping), my closets and my life in general have been filled with pink things.

Life is a funny thing, you know? As I sit here wrapping up this chapter, I just glanced over at the purse caddy in my bedroom to see it solely stacked with black and pink purses, my two favorite colors. There are so many in different shapes and sizes that have been added over the years, that I have actually lost count.

My mother has a habit of buying and distributing gifts on *her* birthday to those she loves. Surprisingly several years ago, she presented me with this large box. As I tore the beautiful pink paper off the box and lifted the lid, low and behold, there was a beautiful pink Michael Kors bag. As I flung it across my shoulder and began to model it in her living room, beaming from ear to ear, I was reminded once again of our Heavenly Father's love for us and how He cares.

He was reminding me, in and through my beautiful mother, that what He has for me is for me. That as a Daughter of The King, all things are possible and what was once unachievable or unattainable has become my reality. He was reminding me that even when I feel unworthy and sometimes second guess myself that He has a marvelous plan for my life and it was wrapped in His purpose.

My purse today is stuffed with all kinds of pink stuff. A pink wallet that holds all my information, a pink telephone which I use to handle business, pink pens which are used to sign contracts and checks, and pink business cards that I use to connect with those around me. If it could talk, it would say, *"Let's go girl, we've got people to see, places to go and a purpose to fulfill.*

While I still appreciate a nice designer handbag, name brands aren't that important to me anymore. In fact, if you looked at my purse collection today you would see a wide mix of designs, many of which have no brand name or label at all. You see my confidence and identity are no longer attached to those things. Today my confidence is rooted in Christ and in knowing that I am the Daughter of the King and through Him I can do and achieve anything.

In addition, I now embrace my new definition of success which is grounded in living a life of significance and positively impacting the lives of those around me.

I have learned that I no longer have to compete or compare myself to others or try and live up to others' expectations of me. I now operate for an audience of One, aiming to please Him and Him alone. If others can get down with it that's great, but if not...oh well. The awesome news is as He did all this for me, He can and wants to do the same for you.

Purse Prayer:

Lord God,

Thank You for reminding me of Your precious love for me and teaching me that I never have to compete and compare myself to others. I am a designer original, custom created for a specific plan and purpose. You have been very intentional about the gifts and talents You have placed within me. Please forgive me for the times I have kept hidden the beautiful treasures within or have taken all the things that set me apart for granted. Please help me fully embrace all the things that make me unique and to fully use my gifts and talents for Your glory.

Amen.

Dr. Nicole Steele

Dr. Nicole Steele is the Founder and Executive Director of Diamond In The Rough Youth Development Program, Inc., an award-winning, faith-based, non-profit mentoring and leadership program which has served nearly 5,000 youth and families since its inception in 2004.

She is also the President of Gem Makers, LLC, which provides program development, consulting, workshops and resources to women, parents and professionals.

In addition, Steele is the Executive Producer and Host of A Priceless Perspective radio, and the published author of two books.

With more than 25 years corporate and youth development experience, Steele has committed her life to empowering women and girls around the world. Dr. Steele is the recipient of multiple awards including The State of Georgia Outstanding Citizen Award and The Presidential Lifetime Achievement Award from President Barak Obama. Steele is convinced that together we can truly transform the world...one child, one family, one community at a time.

I Am...

Courageously walking into the next level of my destiny. I will not abandon my path because the height scares me.

~ DeYonne Parker ~

Chapter 10

The Message In My Mess
By Jamell Cottrell

Finally, I 'm home, whew! It's been a long day. After work I picked up my son and took him to soccer practice. As a single mom I have so much to do and little time to do it. So, I decided to go grocery shopping while he was at practice trying to kill two birds with one stone. And now it's 9:30 pm, it's late but we're home. On my way home, I stopped off and bought myself a strawberry mango smoothie. As my son and I were bringing in the groceries I put my smoothie in my purse, so I wouldn't have to make a trip back to the car. I got in the house put the bags down then noticed my smoothie had spilled in my purse. Ugh! I hate spills!

If my purse could talk it would probably say, *"Girl, look at the mess you've made, but this is nothing compared to the mess you were once in"*. And my response back would be in agreement, *"Yes, purse you are absolutely right!"*

You see there was a time in my life when everything was perfect, so to speak.

I was married with three children, we lived in a beautiful

house and in a nice neighborhood. My husband and I were very active in our church and we both had good jobs. We were in love and had a loving family and our two oldest children were about to go off to college. Life was good; until one day that all changed.

My husband's behavior drastically changed and took me by surprise. He started drinking and having several affairs, which caused serious turbulence in our marriage. Infidelity, lies, and deceit began to consume our marriage and disrupt our home. He stopped answering my calls and didn't come home for days. Eventually, he didn't come home at all because he made an irrational decision to move in with his girlfriend. My home was broken.

Several months later my husband decided he didn't want to be married anymore or have anything to do with our family, so he began the process for a divorce. To make matters worse, he decided to serve me with divorce papers on Christmas day. I couldn't quite understand what I had done to deserve this abrasive treatment from the man that I thought loved me and would spend the rest of my life with.

Reality hit me like a ton of bricks. The good life that I once lived came to an abrupt end and I was now in the beginnings of what I would describe as a full blown storm.

The emptiness, fear and despair that I felt were in intolerable, but no one really knew my pain. The person I loved and who I thought loved me now hated me, turned his back on our family and became my enemy. We argued and fought about everything; there was no common ground between us. Our marriage was failing, and while I tried to fix it, it couldn't be fixed. I tried to make him love me again, but he wouldn't. I prayed that he would come back to us, but he didn't. Instead, I found myself alone and raising my youngest child on my own. I thought, this was not my plan, how am I going to make this work?

It's not easy raising a child alone. Believe me, I know from experience. That was a very difficult season in my life. Seasons come and seasons go, but that winter in my life seemed like it was staying forever.

Spilling that smoothie in my purse forced me to remove all the contents. As I removed the items, I realized that each had a story to tell about that season. If my purse could talk, the tissue would tell how I used it to wipe tears away day after day. The tissue was there to dry my eyes when I was at work, so no one could see me crying. The tissue was in my purse to wipe my tears at church when I was crying out to God to help me and to tell me what to do. The tissue was there for me when I was crying at my son's games because his father didn't come to watch him play. He abandoned our kids and I could see the hurt on their faces. The tissue was there for when I cried for their pain.

If my purse could talk, the lotion would tell of how I used it to cover up that dry season in my life. And sometimes I used my words to cover my dry emotions. I pretended to be happy and put on a fake smile. I told people everything was fine when it wasn't. I was embarrassed and didn't want people to know that I was in a dry place. All the lotion in the world could not cover up my situation.

I reached down to the bottom of my purse and pulled out my lipstick. It was covered with the smoothie. As I was wiping the cold liquid off, I remembered the days I would spend time making myself pretty for him by putting on lipstick. But the reality was that my lips were not the only lips he was kissing.

One night I was praying about my ex-husband, I knew he was out with another woman. In the middle of my crying and telling God what my husband was doing (as if he didn't know) God told me when he gets home I want you to wash his feet. I thought, wash his feet? Why would I do that he doesn't deserve that? I didn't want to do it, but I did. When he got home I took a basin of water, told him to put his feet in it and to relax while I washed his feet. I washed his feet while he went to sleep. That was the most heart wrenching thing I ever done. Tears flowed from my eyes into the water until I could hardly see, but the foot washing wasn't for my ex-husband it was for me. God was humbling me to prepare me for the things he had for me; it was part of the process.

If my purse could talk, the mirror would tell how I would look at my reflection and feel that I was not beautiful or good enough. I couldn't have been or why else would he choose another woman that was much younger than me.

The smoothie leaked into my wallet and as a result, it was wet and sticky. If my wallet could talk, it would tell you about the many sticky situations I was in. The times I didn't have enough money and couldn't pay the mortgage. I had to stretch every dollar to make ends meet. There were times when I didn't have money in my wallet to pay for gas or to buy food. My ex-husband took my name off the credit cards and left me with the bills. I had to, as they say, "rob Peter to pay Paul". I lived from pay check to paycheck and no matter how much I tried to cut back on my expenses there wasn't enough money.

My ex-husband filed for divorce but wouldn't sign the papers. It seems that I was not the only one he lied to. He told his girlfriend he was going to marry her, but he was well aware that he couldn't until the divorce was final. Not signing the papers kept the divorce on hold and provided him with the necessary excuse he needed to not marry her. Since they were always together I had the nauseating experience of being in their presence three times a week for visitations with our youngest son. My life was in shambles and I was the one who had to try to pick up the pieces while he went on to make a new life for himself.

Putting that smoothie in my purse was not a smart idea because my purse was not made to carry a drink. It didn't have a drink holder inside or a pocket deep enough to put it in. I thought it would be safe because it had a lid on it. But the lid only secured the drink when it wasn't standing in an upright position. Being in my purse caused the drink to go sideways just like my marriage. As women, we try to put a lid on our problems to hold things in and we find ourselves doing what we must do to maintain. We keep moving as we pick up the broken pieces along the way. We put our brokenness in a purse, our purse becomes heavy; our purse becomes heavy and we carry the weight of our worries on our shoulders.

There were days when my heart was so heavy that I felt like I couldn't make it another day, but I did. As I look back on those days I'm amazed at how I made it through. It was only by the grace of God. I might have lost my husband and the life I was accustomed to living, but I did not lose my faith. That situation brought me closer to God. I read my bible and had private conversations with God through prayer every day and ach day became a faith walk. I had to trust God just to make it through the day and I was so blessed to have friends that prayed for me during this time. Everyone needs someone to pray for them because there will be days that you won't be able to pray for yourself.

After my ex left us I spent years going back and forth to court fighting for my home and everything in it. At one point he was trying to put me and the kids out on the streets, so he and his girlfriend could move in. My house was about to go into foreclosure and I didn't know it. You see, the court had ordered him to make the payments, but he didn't. Instead he changed the mailing address for the mortgage statements to his job so that I wouldn't know that he wasn't paying the mortgage, in hopes that I would lose the house. When I found out the house payments were so far behind, I couldn't sleep at night thinking about how we could be put out any day. Eventually the mortgage company found out what he did, and they gave me 30 days to catch up on the payments. I didn't have all the money, so they extended it for another month and then another month, this went on for a year.

I stayed in that home without making payments and it never went into foreclosure. No one could do that but God! Then one day God told me to sell it. I didn't want to put it on the market, I loved my home. I told God if this is really what you want me to do then let the house sell in 30 days. If it doesn't sell in 30 days, I'll take it off the market and know that it's not what you're telling me to do. My house sold one hour after I put it on the market! I was able to sell the house for the full market price which was great, but I had to split the sell with my ex-husband because we were still legally married. To tell you the truth, I struggled with that. For him to receive money from a house that he abandoned and tried to put us out of, just didn't seem fair. But that was just a stepping stone for what God had for me. Since that time, I have purchased three homes.

I was in a battle in many ways. I was engaged in a battle that I was not equipped to fight, and in court things where starting to go his way. He had an attorney and I didn't. I felt like I couldn't afford one. God spoke to me and said, "this is a spiritual battle, every battle requires a fight". I told God, "I don't want to fight, you know it's not my nature to fight. He spoke to me and said, "I didn't say you had to fight you just have to get dressed for the battle and show up to watch me fight." You see we don't have to fight every battle we just have to get dressed for the battle by putting on the whole armor of God and show up for the fight. God will fight our battles.

God will prepare us for the things we go through if we follow His instructions. My instruction was to trust God and hire an attorney. I didn't realize it at the time, but that was part of dressing for the battle and when I did God took it from there. You should have seen the look on my ex-husbands face when I showed up in the court room with my attorney! Things quickly began to turn in my favor and I was able to pay my attorney and to this day I don't know how I did it, but I did.

Eventually, I won that battle. The judge granted me

everything. It took four long years for my ex-husband to sign the papers to finalize the divorce and it didn't happen until I heard God tell me to move to another state. "What move to another state? I can't do that!" I said out loud, but, I did. That was a big step for me. A move that required me to use faith in spite of my fears even though I was scared and uncertain about my future. But in spite of my fears I made a bold move. My youngest son and I left my extended family, my eldest son and everything I had in California and moved to Georgia. I didn't know anyone there except my daughter and her family.

While the move seemed unthinkable at one-point, things began to fall in place and that transition changed my life for the better. I discovered who I was and how relentless God created me to be. I got a fresh start and a new life. I had a new house that I built, I bought new furniture and a new car I had wanted for years. I drove that car off the lot, paid in full. I met new people and developed new friendships. Everything around me was new. When God gives you a new beginning it's a wonderful thing! Three months after I moved, my ex-husband signed the divorce papers and I was finally free from that marriage; it felt good to be free.

In all that I went through God was with me, I couldn't have made it without him. I have so many testimonies of God's goodness and grace upon me at that time. If my purse could talk from the inside out, it would tell you about where I am today. I have more now than I had before. My children and grandchildren are good, and I am happy and blessed. I am an overcomer and a survivor. Through adversity I became stronger, wiser, resilient and self-reliant. I'm no longer vulnerable, I am valuable!

No one can put a price on you and no man can take away your self-worth unless you give them the power. Now, I can say I know me, love me and love being me. I couldn't say that before because I wasn't living for me, I was living for someone else. I learned that I could do what I thought I couldn't do. That's why throughout this story you've heard me say, "But, I did".

Sometimes the hard things we go through in life feel like it's the end, but it's not. When I was dealing with the suffering and the loss all I could think of was what I was going through. I couldn't begin to imagine me living in another state, owning another home, and living a better life. But, I did. I had no idea that God was doing great things for me while I was in the dark. God has a greater plan for our lives, but we have to go through the process. Process doesn't always feel good, but it's necessary for our growth.

God has a picture of what he has for us when we complete the process, but in order for us to see that picture, we have to be developed. Our character, our patience and our faith have to be developed. And just like pictures, these things can only be developed in the dark.

Some of my greatest moments with God happened when I was in a dark place. It was all part of the process. It's easy to trust God when the world you live in is sunny and bright, but can you trust him in the dark?

I have forgiven my ex-husband for all the things he did that drastically affected all of us. God teaches us that we are to forgive others as He forgives us. When I forgave him I felt a release from condemnation, guilt and shame. Forgiveness is not for the other person it is for you. In this life, trials will come but you have what it takes to overcome them if you just tap into who you really are. The devil will tell you that your nothing he will tell you're a failure, but don't believe his lies. There is so much more inside of you and he knows it.

The devil knows what you're capable of but he doesn't know your full potential. You must know when it comes to him you have the upper hand. He will lay all the facts before you but just because it's a fact doesn't mean it's the truth. The fact was my marriage was failing and I was going through a bad divorce and not feeling very loved. But the truth was I was victorious, and my life would get better and I was loved. At some time or another you will go through a storm. When that time comes hold on to the boat even if you have to ride into the shore on broken pieces; you will make it. Two things I learned during that storm is that I was smarter and stronger than I thought I was. Storms come to make you stronger, to make you wiser, to change your character, and to build your faith. You won't find out what you're made of until you go through a storm. God doesn't want the storms to destroy us, He wants to make us whole while the devil will tell you that you won't make it through the storm. Don't look at the storm, keep your eyes on Jesus and He will bring you through. You are a daughter of the King, you are loved, and you can do all things through Christ who gives you strength. (Phil 4:13)

The storm is not there to take you out; it comes to bring you into the goodness of God. If God allowed the storm to come in your life, He has the power to control the storm and if God lives in you, you have that same power. So, ride the waves knowing that God is with you and you have the victory. You will make it, you're stronger than you think. The next time the devil tells you you're in a storm and you won't make it tell the devil," I don't know what you're talking about devil, I am the storm"!

<u>*Purse Prayer:*</u>

Though the challenges of life may come like a raging storm, father I pray that You will keep my sister in the palm of Your hand. Give her grace to ride the waves give her wisdom in her uncertainty and give her peace in the midst of her storm. Show her Your love Father. Walk with her for You said You will never leave her or forsake her. May her faith be grounded in You. No matter what it looks like, You have the final say over her life and You have a better plan. Speak to her situation Lord and turn it around for her good and for Your glory.

Yet what we suffer now, is nothing compared to the glory he will reveal to us later. (Romans 8:18 NLT)

Jamell Cottrell

Jamell is a leader, teacher and coordinator and owner of By Design Logistics LLC. Her passion is coordinating the logistics for events. Jamell is known as a woman of strong faith. She has walked through the fire and weathered many storms. She is a prayer warrior and intercessor and when she speaks God's word it comes to pass. A native of Southern California, Jamell now resides in Georgia. She has a desire to help women and has spent most of her life encouraging women and speaking life into their souls.

Being a divorced mother, Jamell has a special place in her heart for single women and single moms. She understands their struggles and their needs.

Over the years Jamell has served in her community and church. She has volunteered with the Diamond In the Rough Youth Development Program for over 11 years as the Single Moms Coordinator and Prayer Team Leader.

1 Am...

Free to let go of my past and fully
Embrace my future. No longer am

1 incarcerated by my mistakes and missteps.
1 am *Uncaged.*

~ DeYonne Parker ~

Chapter 11

Clean Out Your Purse

By Dr. Natoshia Anderson

You know, I didn't really carry a purse until I graduated college. I always had a wallet and maybe a little pouch that looked like a purse, but never one of those purses that looked like a purse. I couldn't or didn't understand the need for one. They are bulky and heavy. One of my girlfriends had a purse so heavy that she eventually started having to see a chiropractor about back issues! One night, we pulled at least $10 to $12 in change out of her purse, not to mention the wallet, the notebook, the make-up case, the books, keys, and miscellaneous items that were in that purse. Whew!! It was a lot. What would *I* put in one? Little did I know that I would, over time, become just like my friend.

I believe the reason I didn't carry a purse for so long was because I was carrying all my stuff internally. I didn't really need an outward showing of all my stuff. This meant that I didn't know how to let it go and then, to have some outward showing of needing something or someone else to help me carry the load wasn't cool with me AT ALL.

154

I started off with a book bag in college and graduated to a briefcase I carried to work each day. Then I thought, "I don't want to carry the briefcase when I go out to lunch or the after-work errands." I got a small purse, but it wasn't big enough to carry all the essentials that I had spread out in the briefcase. So, I bought my first "big purse".

The idea behind a purse is to have something to keep all the things you think you are going to need in one place while you're out. They make them small, medium and large and even extra-large. There are name brands and generic brands. There are so many different brands and makes of purses.

Purses are now their own category in the clothing arena. My favorite types of purses are the ones with little to no compartments on the inside. My girlfriends call it a "dump bag." I want to be able to see everything and not have to search various compartments to find things. Dump all my stuff in there and let them get to know each other.

What's in the dump bag? Everything!!! Over time my purse became sooooo heavy to carry. I can remember my husband picking it up one day and wondering how I was able to carry that around every day. I wanted to say "Exactly, I carry this around EVERY SINGLE DAY!"

In my bag, all areas were bleeding into one another. Since there are no boundaries or compartments in the dump bag, everything, all my unresolved issues, problems, and situations were right there waiting anytime I opened that bag.

Contents of the "Dump Bag"

I have always felt a little different from the rest of my family. I knew from an early age I wasn't going to do "normal" things. I just knew. Maybe that was the God in me letting me know early on that I wasn't going to be the kid that would just fall in line. Boy, was that ever true. I was the little girl that asked a lot of questions and kept asking them until my mother would tell me to keep my mouth closed but keep my ears open.

People would get annoyed at me for having 5,000 questions and for being curious. After all, during the time I was growing up, kids were seen and not heard. I was the kid that would get a toy and immediately want to know how it worked. I broke so many toys trying to figure out how they worked.

My mom and dad called me the most destructive kid they had. I was always trying something different because I had this inherent desire to KNOW. This led me down vastly different pathways from my sister and from my other family members. To this day, there is still a need for me KNOW things. I've had experiences that have enhanced this need.

One such experience happened when I was 11 years old. I was molested by a man who married into our family. This experience changed my life in a myriad of ways. Over the span of one year, I went from being a moderately happy preteen, to a confused and inwardly lonely "tweener" who just knew that no one would understand what had happened to her.

In my efforts to understand what was happening to me, I did my 7th grade science fair project on childhood sexual abuse. My social studies/science teacher didn't get it either and I wasn't in a place where I could explain it to her. She told me that "these types of projects never win." That was quite alright with me. I'd done the research just for myself.

I can remember my mother being aghast that I was taking on this subject for my project. She kept asking me about this choice. Did I have anything that I wanted to tell her? Nope!!! The abuser told me that I would destroy my family if I told. What child wants or needs that responsibility? I eventually did tell, and it did destroy a family, but not mine. The abuser's marriage to my family member went downhill from there. They got divorced and he moved away. The abuse stopped but I was still left broken, confused, and scared.

While it was not my fault that a family was destroyed, I carried this responsibility in my dump bag for a long time. The research suggests that there is psychological, physical, emotional, and mental damage done to children who endure abuse. These girls can suffer from anxiety, depression, nightmares, and low self-esteem. They can also struggle with trusting others, intimacy, and sexual relationships. I'm no psychologist for sure, however I can speak from my experience and tell you that it changed me.

I've had many years of counseling and have done A LOT of research in this area just trying to understand and feed my need to know why. Make no mistake about it, abuse of any kind changes who you are. IT FOREVER CHANGES WHO YOU ARE!

One of the things that I've learned along the way about those who have been abused, myself included, is that we are hoarders. Hoarders of hurt. Many of us feel that no one will understand our pain, our confusion, OUR HURT. It *is* very real and raw. Thus, we hoard the hurt. We keep it hidden. The hurt becomes something else we put in the dump bag. Because there is no place else it CAN go.

There are still times when I think back on the sheer amount of hurt and confusion surrounding that time. I often wonder how I made it through with a clear mind to become a whole person.

Another thing I've grown to know is that this experience changed the way I viewed myself and my body. I was always an awkward girl growing up. I was tall, skinny, wore glasses, had long arms, etc. I didn't know what to do with myself. I hadn't quite figured out how *to be* yet. I didn't really understand all that was happening in my body.

I can remember thinking there was something physically wrong with me when my breasts started to grow in...What is that? I'm not sure what I thought that experience would be, but the one I had was NOT IT.

When I was molested, it just tripled my awkwardness. I thought everybody knew or they could see that there was something different about me. I'm not sure I've ever viewed myself as a victim of child abuse, but I surely understood then and understand now that it was wrong and that it was something that should not have ever happened to me. It colored my view of myself, just at the time when I was still discovering who I was.

I could never really reconcile what happened to me and to who I thought I was. Somehow, I started to believe that there was something about me that led this individual to think that it was okay to manipulate me in this way. That it was okay to change my world view before it had fully formed. That I LET HIM!!!

This guilt and warped view led to many bad decisions during my teen years and into adulthood. I believed wholeheartedly that I couldn't and didn't trust myself much less anyone else. Yep, that's in the bag too.

Relationships with the opposite sex were tough for me. Dating during my teenage and young adult years were awkward. I could never figure out if the boy really liked me or it it was the mask I wore every day that he liked. Since I couldn't trust him or me, it was tough to decipher his motivation for wanting to be with me and I wasn't going to ask. That would leave me too vulnerable.

Sex was a no go. I couldn't wrap my head around what it was really supposed to be. But eventually, I decided that I wanted to give it a try. I didn't get the hype. Was I doing it wrong? Was this all it was? If so, then I could do without it! All it brought me was anxiety and doubt. Another thing to place in the dump bag.

Self-doubt is insidious and vicious. It never leaves you alone. It's the devils' voice in the back of your mind telling you that you're rotten, that you'll never amount to anything, that everyone will blame you when they find out what happened to you, it was your fault, you're supposed to feel bad. You can't make good decisions from this space.

I thought having friends or a boyfriend meant that I had to accept being treated as less than, ignored, cheated on, talked to disrespectfully, and diminished. It meant I wasn't good enough and I continued to strive to be "good enough." It's a tough way to live, I know I tried. One more thing to add to the dump bag. You can NEVER please others this way, even if that is your motivation.

Time To Clean Out That Purse

You know, I never really understood that bible verse that said that we are to be cheerful givers until much recently in my life. I also wouldn't have understood the gospel song that says "I give myself away" in the sense that they meant it. I gave myself away cheerfully and willfully to others without really knowing who it was I was giving away. In giving myself way, it meant that I was stressed out, burned out, wore out, and tired.

One of the best books I have read in my life is called "How Full is Your Bucket?" by Tom Rath. In this book the author uses a metaphor of the bucket and dipper. He tells the reader that we all have a bucket that is filled each day. In the bucket are ourselves, gifts, talents, abilities, capabilities, attitudes, opinions, beliefs, thoughts, experiences, etc. These are things that we give away each day to others. Some we give willingly, meaning we give people permission to dip in our buckets; but others take.

If we are willingly giving and others are taking, our buckets, will soon be empty whether we like it or not. The question then becomes, who's refilling our buckets and how do we stop those from taking from us?

I read this book at the right time. It gives simple strategies to help you keep your bucket full and know when your bucket is being dipped from. My bucket was being dipped from and I didn't know or didn't recognize it, and I was giving myself away to the wrong people. I forgot about myself in the busyness of life. I got married, had kids, lost myself in my marriage and with being a mother. I lost myself in my career. I lost myself in doing the things that I believed I should be doing at this stage in my life. I didn't recognize my own worth and couldn't see my value. My dump bag was FULL!!!

All this stuff, in my bag, sitting next to each other. Getting acquainted with each other. Can you imagine carrying all of this around? It was so unnecessarily heavy and what's worse was that I couldn't find anything in it!!! So how did I know when it was time to clean out my dump bag? It was one particular incident that struck a deep chord in my soul.

My daughter had an experience at her cushy private school that ultimately let me know that I needed to deal with my own issues. She was inappropriately touched by a boy in her class. At this time, my daughter was three maybe four years old. She had the mind to tell her teacher about what happened. I would have liked to believe that this was something kind of innocent, but my mind wouldn't let me! The school calls to let me know that this occurred. I LOST MY MIND!

"Not my daughter! Not my daughter! NO, NO, not her, not her, not her!" I'm crying. You know, the Oprah ugly cry; I'm doing a stellar job at recreating that. I couldn't function anymore. I don't remember how I got from my office to the school. I do remember that the headmaster wanted to talk to me when I arrived at the school, but I JUST COULDN'T. I remember hugging my daughter so tight and apologizing for not protecting her. Meanwhile, she grabbed my face with both hands, kissed my lips and said, "I love you Mommy." I smiled a teary smile at her and I knew in that moment that I had to be better, if I was going to be a good mother and an even better person.

Let It Go!

Have you ever had your purse drop and the contents fall out? How many of you have found items you had been looking for when that happens? Raise your hand. How many of you found items you didn't even know was lost in the first place, but you're happy you found them? Raise your hand. How many of you found stuff you didn't know was in there? Yeah, raise your hand here too. That's the thing about a purse, it holds it all. And it will hold all that stuff until you are ready to let it go.

The whole purpose of the book, aptly named, "You are a Badass: How to Stop Doubting Your Greatness and Start Living an Awesome Life," by Jen Sincero, is to remind you that you are AWESOME AND AMAZING. I make a conscious effort to remind myself of this every day. No matter what has happened to you or me. No matter what you've done or allowed to happen, no matter what you think about yourself right now, YOU ARE AWESOME. I AM AWESOME!

God does not make mistakes. You and I are not mistakes. Our life is as it is because God said so. Believe that you are great. That your life is great and that you are destined to do great things. You have got to love yourself. I love myself.

If I am to believe that I am great and amazing, I must get rid of the old stuff that says that I'm just the opposite. I must get rid of the old make-up that was covering up my flawed beauty, dried out pens used to erase my story, crinkled candy wrappers that represent the sweet nothings of unfulfilled promises and dreams, various receipts from past purchases that are representatives of questionable choices and old ideas I've had about myself, bobbie pins used to cover up my real hair, and miscellaneous items that represent all the stuff that I just haven't dealt with. I think it's time for me to let it go and clean out my purse

Is It Time For A New Purse?

So, I'm sure some of you are asking "how do I go about cleaning out the contents of my purse when I have so much in it?" I'm glad you asked! It's going to take some work on your behalf, but let me help you.

ONE. Dump out the contents, if that works best for you. Meaning, the stuff you've been carrying around in your heart. Take each item out one by one. Look at all the "stuff" you've been holding on to. Aren't you amazed at it all? I know I was. Didn't know you were still holding on to that old hurt, that old experience? Didn't know you still had those unbecoming beliefs about yourself? Didn't know that you were still holding grudges against folks? Yeah, I didn't either. Still wondering why you aren't farther along in life or in your career? Look at what's in your purse.

If you are to believe and trust fully in the God of the Universe, believe that He wants more for you than your current situation. He wants you living your best life, putting forth goodness in the Universe. I'm not saying that it will be easy. It will be quite the opposite. It will hurt and be painful even, but the end WILL BE glorious. Yes, clean out that purse!

TWO. Since you now know that you are awesome, and God wants good things for you, you might consider getting a new purse. You have the right to live your best life. Give yourself permission to be great. Make no excuses for being great. The genuine people that are in your life for the right reasons will be happy for you and will encourage you. Surround yourself with people who will tell you the truth and call you on your crap. You need good people, those who will hold you accountable to be the greatest you can be. The ones who want the best for you. Clean out your purse!

THREE. While you're cleaning out your purse, it's time to get real with yourself. Pull out that mirror and take a good hard look at yourself. Be willing to tell yourself the truth. The hard-dirty truth. Own your own stuff. You know the ugly stuff. The stuff you deny when confronted by others. We are all works in progress. There are things that we all must work on. Take the time to get to the heart of the matter. What's your truth?

My truth is that my trust issues might have stemmed from what happened to me in the past, but at some point, I claimed it and allowed mistrust to permeate my world. I had to clean that out. It took a lot of work and if I'm being totally transparent, it's still something that I struggle with. I clean out my purse often. Don't project your stuff onto other people. People who are close to us are often mirrors of ourselves showing us areas of improvement. It's true that God uses people and situations to assist us in being better people. Clean out your purse!

FOUR. Now, let's really do some cleaning and truth telling. You know you have some people in your corner that shouldn't be. Am I right? You know the ones I'm talking about. They've outgrown their welcome. Their purpose is over and past. You need to let them go. I'm not saying that it's easy or fun, but they must go. They're now detrimental to you living your best life. Clean out your purse!!

You don't need those things that used to fill the void you felt in your heart. They no longer serve the purpose they once did. You no longer need that thing, object, person, or situation. It's not relevant to your story anymore. Yes, that painful situation may have happened, and you may have been affected, but it's not your end. God is too great and too strong, and He promised that He wouldn't leave nor forsake you. He cares too much to leave you like this. Clean that purse out.

Sometimes getting a new purse is the start of a transformation. My girlfriends tell me that they smile at the THOUGHT of a new purse. Imagine that! Just the thought of something new is something to smile about. Start anew. Reminisce, review or grieve and throw it away. Replenish those things you need and KNOW just as God loves you (and your new purse too) you have the right to love yourself fiercely, loyally, and unapologetically.

Purse Prayer:

Lord, You are amazing. Your grace and mercy are sufficient in my life. You are the keeper of my soul and I love You with my whole heart. You are a way maker and promise keeper. There is no one above you. Lord, clean my purse. Remove those things that are not of You from my life. Take from me those who would do me harm. Give me clarity so that I may see with new eyes who is for me and those that are against me. Gird me Lord, as I move towards You and away from those things, situations, and people, that won't allow me to be great, to shine in honor of You. Allow me to be washed anew in my knowledge of You and to become more like You. Allow my light to become a beacon for others to want to know You. These things I ask in Your Name. AMEN.

Dr. Natoshia Anderson

Dr. Natoshia Anderson, CEO of Smart STEM, LLC., has a genuine love of teaching and learning and is fully vested in the advancement of STEM Education.

She has a Bachelor of Science degree in Mechanical Engineering Technology from Southern Polytechnic State University, an MBA with a specialization in Marketing in 2006 and a Doctor of Education in Educational Leadership in 2010 from the University of Phoenix.

She holds a deep and abiding love for women in general, and women of color specifically, and wants to see these groups succeed and win.

Professionally, Dr. Natoshia is an entrepreneur whose company focuses on curriculum development and professional development for teachers in STEM, and research in STEM education. She is also a wife of 19 years and mother of two amazing teenagers.

I Am...

a beautiful representation of God's love.
I walk in my *Power* and *Purpose* and
I'm not afraid to fully embrace the divine
assignments that my heavenly Father has
placed on my life.

- DeYonne Parker -

Chapter 12

Shar's Harmony

By Shermaine "Shar" Marshall

Hi there, I'm Shar's Harmony Purse! Come on in, have a seat and grab your favorite beverage because I'm about to share the details of my purse life story with my owner, Shar. It's going to require a little imagination on your part and a lot of heartfelt understanding. Ready? Here we go.

One night my owner was is in a deep sleep and suddenly awakened by a voice she heard close by. As she rubbed her eyes to get an unobstructed vision around her room, she noticed her purse on the chair by the closet. She got up and walked towards the door to see who was in her house. The closer she got to the door, the louder the voice seemed to be. She looked around and then realized the voice was coming from the direction where her purse was located.

Initially she thought it was a dream until she heard another sound and immediately recognized that the commotions were coming from inside her purse (that's me...lol). The room became silent for a few moments, which made her believe that she was now fully awake, but as she turned to walk back toward her bed, she heard the voice from her purse declare: *"Jesus, build a fence around my owner today. She needs You Father, for she knows not what she needs with all this stuff inside of me. She has ruined my figure."* Shar began to tremble, and then quickly sprung into her bed, thinking to herself again, *"I must be delusional because I know purses do not talk."*

Shar didn't quite know what to make of this other than she had to be sleep walking...so she returned back to her bed. As she stared at the ceiling, her heart began to go from pounding to a steady pace and she slowly drifted back into a deep sleep.

The items inside of me run deep. Beneath the murky linings, lie hidden treasures that only my owner and I can see. Oh, my goodness I'm bursting at the seams. Why am I so heavy and bulky? I need to look around a bit more to see what these hidden treasures are inside of me that my owner has graciously overstuffed me with. As I peep out of my zippered opening, I look around to see if she has a larger purse she can dump all of these contents into because there is just no more room to stuff anything else inside of me. I am afraid if she stuffs anything else in me I may completely fall apart and everything will end up on the floor. Unfortunately, my owner has too many purses too choose from, so I will ride it out and pray she does not add anything else inside of me.

What's in the Purse?

Some women grab everything they can and drop it in their purse before they leave the house. It seems to be the most crucial thing to do before closing the door and throwing us on the front seat or floor before getting in the car and closing the door.

As I look around and observe the contents that Shar has placed inside me, I can't help but wonder why she has a real address book with over 800 names and addresses! Does anyone have a tangible address book in 2018? Surely, she knows that technology has made it possible to never have to write a number or address down again! While continuing to rummage through my murky linings, another hidden treasure is revealed; she has several ink pens. Yes, ink pens! There are enough ink pens to supply a middle school! Where is she going with all these pens? Maybe she has them in here to write down her deepest thoughts, because she loves writing. She often carries a journal around with her; so her ink pens are put to good use.

While maneuvering items to view what else is in my fake designer interior, I discover a small black purse. Now who does that? A purse inside of a purse. Wait a minute, what is all of this in this in here...is it make-up! My owner has enough make-up in the small black purse to apply make-up to ten faces. Is there a new pill on the market yet for this kind of insane craziness? She also has a bottle of what looks like red fingernail polish and it's turned upside down. It looks like the inscription written on it is something about lipstick, but I am totally confused because it's in a nail polish bottle (I think this is that new lipstick by that singer whose name is difficult to pronounce). Now wait a minute! You're not going to believe the next item...Lemon Pepper Seasoning! Why on earth does she have Lemon Pepper Seasoning in her purse, Lord? "Why?" Why?" Why?"

After completing my thorough investigation of the contents within my inner lining, I came to an embarrassing realization. I did not see any money or loose change tucked inside. Could I have missed it? Or could it be inside of one of these other compartments? All that was in plain sight was that dreadful address book, ink pens, a journal, make-up, a nail polish bottle that contains lipstick and lemon pepper seasoning. How crazy is this to carry around a $300.00 fake designer bag with no money, but have lemon pepper seasoning? If there's another compartment in here that contains a chicken wing, I swear I will have to find a new owner.

Purse Ties

It's amazing how many people, places and things relate to women's purses. It seems the older the woman; the bigger and heavier the purse. Admittedly, my owner is no different because she grabbed the aforementioned items, dropped them inside of me and rolled out the house. She can get pretty uptight if she discovers she has forgotten something at home. One of her favorite colloquialisms she often whispers to herself is, "*It's better to have and not need than need and not have.*" I guess I have no choice in the matter, because she continues to drop things inside of me and I get fatter and fatter.

Additionally, my owner hates borrowing other people's things, so that's another reason why she carries everything. I noticed however, one thing she never leaves home without is her cell phone, including the cell phone chargers and three or four charging cords. She also keeps two bottles of hand sanitizer handy at all times. She keeps one for herself and one for others to use. Concisely, I am more like her security blanket.

Peace In Memorable Pain (P.I.M.P.)

So, now that you know what's inside of me, what does this all mean? What's the significance of the items inside of me? I truly believe that each of these items (umm...except for the lemon pepper seasoning) has a special meaning in my owner's life. For instance, she journals about everyone in her life. Her mom, brothers, father, stepfather, husband, children, grandmothers, her closest friends, her past life and mainly GOD. Journaling is a part of her healing process and a parallel to her cries. I hear her sometimes when we are in the car whispering and sometimes shouting out, *"God, I know You hear me. I know You can stop this pain. I know You can give me peace about the void in my heart."*, and she often writes the same in her journal. The void she writes about is in regards to missing her babies and wishing she could see them again.

Shar has a 33-year-old son, a 26-year-old daughter and sadly, she buried her youngest son 8 years ago. He was shot 5 times in New Orleans, on July 19, 2010 and died from his gunshot wounds. In her journal you can find several entries that read, "I miss my babies and one day I will see them again." Although my owner is bubbly, sociable, respected and loved, she is desperately masking her pain. When she's alone sometimes she cries so hard that her tears flood her pillows like a category five hurricane.

Yesterday my owner placed a prayer card under her make-up bag. The prayer card is for her deceased son and she has carried it for 8 years now. That same card resides in the cover of her cell phone. She placed it in these visible places as a constant reminder for her to never turn her phone off or never be in a place where she doesn't have good reception. Her heart can't handle a repeat of what happened to her beloved son.

Take a deep breath as I attempt to walk you through the

details of that devastating event, as I remember it.

On the night of July 18, 2010, Shar spent the night at a friend's house around the corner from her job. She never liked being alone at home. That night, she and her friend ate dinner, laughed, discussed relationships, both current and past, and then she prepared for bed. For some odd reason she could not get comfortable that night. Shar was wide awake and tossed and turned all night. Her girlfriend went off to sleep, while Shar played around with her phone but lost the signal. The area where her girlfriend lived had poor cell phone reception, but she always told her husband that if he couldn't reach her, "make sure to call her girlfriend since her phone seemed to have no issues with reception." She told the same thing to her son Jermaine and her daughter Jasmine that live in Atlanta, but she never reiterated that to her youngest son in New Orleans. They spoke occasionally because he lived with his father.

In the fateful early morning hours of July 19, 2010, there was a knock on the door. Her girlfriend yelled from the back room, "Shar your husband's at the door!" Shar woke up not suspecting a thing. As she opened the door, her husband bypassed her, when any other time he would grab her and hug and kiss her with playfulness. This time was different. He walked towards the fireplace, then turned and faced her with tears in his eyes.

She ran over to him and asked him what was wrong. He responded that he received a call from New Orleans Homicide. She just stared at him thinking something happened to her ex-husband who her son Lil Leo lived with. She said again, "Baby are you ok?" She was feeling and touching all over his body to make sure nothing was hurting him. He said "Baby, baby, New Orleans Homicide called". This time his words stuck and she froze in her steps. Shar began to scream, a piercing scream. The scream was so loud it sounded like glass shattering. It was as if her breath was leaving her body. Her screams got louder and louder as her husband explained that the New Orleans Homicide detectives called, and Lil Leo was shot and pronounced dead at the scene.

The silence and screams at the same time were deafening. The torrential downpour was as if God himself had turned on a gushing water faucet from her eyes. It was the saddest and most devastating moments she had ever experienced.

Shar reached into the bottom of my lining and pulled out a pack of cigarettes. She walked outside into the darkness, lit a cigarette, grasped her journal, looked up to the sky and again screamed as loud as she could. This was a heavy weight of sadness that my owner now had to endure.

To add to an already sad situation, my owner later found out that her son was trying to call her that night, but could not reach her, so her husband got the phone call. For this reason, she does not turn off her cell phone. She cannot bear to not be in contact with her other two children or her husband, parents, siblings or friends.

Shar carries a lot in me because she carries a lot in her memory. She is very conscious of being connected and having the things and people she needs to feel safe and secure. She prays daily and still mentions her deceased son's name when she speaks of her children. She will never lose the thought of him because he is a part of her even if he is no longer physically here.

When a parent, grandparent, sibling, or even a friend dies, it's a different kind of pain than that of losing a child suddenly. My owner knows this pain a little too well. Prior to losing her son, Lil Leo, she miscarried a son in her seventh month of pregnancy and never got a chance to say goodbye. So you see, all those pens really do serve a deeper purpose. She needs them to write down all the painful loss she has experienced so she has a place to put it other than just in her heart.

I've been a part of my owner's life for many years She is my rightful owner. I've not only been with her through the sorrows of losing her beloved sons, but I've also seen her experience the triumphs of becoming an accomplished make-up artist and business owner. I have housed many of her precious journals and stored her numerous ink pens. I have protected her beloved address book and kept her make-up intact. I have heard her prayers and cries and even provided the tissue needed to at least wipe the physical evidence from her face. Now someone needs to help lighten her load because she is holding on to things in me that need to be removed.

I often say to myself, "Let go and let God, Shar".

As she comes back in from outside and approaches me, throws the pack of cigarettes inside of me and closes me up; I hear her praying for peace and that God's will be done.

Purse Prayer:

Dear God,

I am still here to hear Your voice daily. I sing a Harmony in my heart daily because of who You have made me and how You have shaped me. As I reminisce on the blessings in my life, I sing the Harmony You put in me and that is why I am grateful for this chapter title, Shar's Harmony. God, Your Word reminds me to, "Arise and shine, for your light has come and the glory of the LORD rises upon you." (Isaiah 60:1 NIV). I finally hear my Harmony. I am wiser, stronger, fearless and capable of trusting You with everything in my life. I cannot be without You in my life, for my life is empty without Your presence. I trust You with my joy and pain. I know that with each 24-hour day You are with me, so I humbly say thank You for loving me enough. Your grace has kept me, and your mercy has sustained me. I want to thank you for this journey and for my parents, siblings, and friends. I thank you for Dee Parker and the vision You gave her for this project. I thank You for Alicia Ward for introducing me to Dee Parker, and the other incredible authors on this journey. Most of all to Christopher L.L. Marshall, my awesome husband and my amazing children, Jermaine Alsion, Thomas, Jasmine LaShay Vanderhorst and Leo Harmon Vanderhorst, Jr. (RIP) for with them, my life has changed incredibly for the best. Thank you for all of our purse confessions as we become free and to get closer to you and learn how to trust you authentically and wholeheartedly. This is Shar's Harmony, singing daily.

In Jesus' holy, Name, Amen.

Shermaine "Shar" Marshall

Shermaine Marshall, a seasoned Human Resources professional with over 30 years of corporate experience, earned an Associate's Degree in Business Administration from the University of Phoenix in 2010. When Shar's teenage son, Leo, was unexpectedly killed her pursuit of education was put on the back burner. With God's grace upon her, Shar was able to recover and fulfill the promise she made to her children as she went on to earn her Bachelor's Degree in 2016 from Bellevue University.

After her 4th lay off from her 32 year corporate career, she made the decision to finally surrender all to God and pursued her purpose. As a result *Changing Faces Make-up Artistry (CFMUA)* was born! The mission and goal of CFMUA is not to just create another beautiful face but to also create a beautiful person to match from the inside out!

I Am...

Ready to help others *Redefine* their definition of me. I am a *Beautiful* story.

~ DeYonne Parker ~

Chapter 13

My Pursonality

(My Life Inside A Handbag)

By Dr. Cynthia Harper

Inevitably, I have always been drawn to purses with a structured form; like an old- fashioned lunch box but with compartments to store my personal items. Referring to them as handbags defines them as a functional piece of art. For an example, my leopard bag is a classic . . . always in style. It roars to primal fashion instinct.

Oh, but the black leather is contemporary, sleek and chic. But my favorite is my red leather bag, it makes a bold statement of power, truly an expressionistic creation.

Generally, I gravitate to handbags that have short straps, small to medium in size and with non-collapsing sides. Very similar to the way I like to live my life - organized.

My leopard bag is primarily adorned in the winter. Because it's oversized, furry and exotic, it certainly catches people's attention and they often say, "That is a beautiful purse ma'am". The downfall of this "fabulous fashion piece" is that the latch is magnetic and does not always close securely. Once while exiting a plane, I did not realize it was open and consequently the contents fell out. I was slightly embarrassed not just because of the contents of the bag, but because it brought the passengers following behind me to a standstill. Initially, I thought "no big deal", but the piercing stares penetrated the very essence of my soul. Though most looks were kind, it revealed to me that I had over-packed my purse.

Scavenging in the crevices of a Jetway ramp is just not cute! As people began to walk around me, I felt a little uncomfortable. I had red, hot pink, gold, clear gloss and a myriad of lipsticks rolling around. Though my lipsticks are very pertinent to me, my eye-lashes are my thing and I had multiple packs of them looking up at me, not to mention coins, pens and earrings. Nevertheless, I was traveling and brought my extra, you know, "that just in case stuff." The operative word here is "extra."

I need to share with you my friend, that you alone...are enough. Don't overly concern yourself with intense looks, sly whispers and other's stinking-thinking of you; that's their business. There is no need to fear "being extra" or for that matter anything else. Let them stare when you drop something or even when you fall, don't adhere to the pressures of life. Being secure exemplifies your radiance, being imperfect illustrates your humbleness and being you demonstrates your authenticity. Get back up! Remember, "If you faint in the day of adversity, your strength is small." (Proverbs 24:10).

Oh...if that leopard bag would have spoken at that time, it would have roared, loud and clear, God, the promise keeper, has kept his promise. I have been delivered from a desert place and know devil in hell, can separate me from the love of God. After all, I had survived a long valley period where I was in a dry place. I realized that if I could weather the storm of losing everything I owned, and came back stronger than before, why worry about things falling out of my purse. My natural inclination is flair, not frivolous but sophisticated; I am a girlie-girl and I enjoy "extra!" People often confuse confidence with arrogance or big personalities with egotism but when you seek and strive after the characteristics of God, He sets you free to be you.

One of my favorite proverbs is, "Hope deferred makes the heart sick, but a longing fulfilled is a tree of life" (Proverbs, 13:12). He is restoring me as He will you. When you have periods of trouble in your life, promise me that when you are feeling down you will keep something in your purse, wallet or in your heart to remind yourself that you will survive that experience.

Friends, while handbags are receptacles designed to carry

things, let's not carry the unnecessary weight of other people's opinions. Let it go! Whatever you are carrying in life that you don't need and is not pertinent, ask God to take it. Jesus was crucified on the cross for us and we don't have to carry all the unexpected changes in life with us. We all deserve to be set-free. Unnecessary burdens are senseless, they weigh us down. One or two tubes of lipstick could have been sufficient for me to carry, but I chose to carry "extra." In fact, I only used one shade when I was home, the matte hot pink. What or who are you carrying that you need to eliminate? I suggest you think about what you need to stop carrying, and if you think it - ink it. Once it's written, find a trash receptacle and deposit it there. Begin your process of a lighter burden by seeking help, bury those things and never looking back.

All Things Black

For many people, the color black is a huge part of their wardrobe. Shoes, garments, belts, little black dresses, jeans and everything in between. While I have many black bags, my favorite is the well-made sleek and chic. I don't use it often, but when I do, I know it's on point. It was a nice gift and I am grateful to have it. The compartments are perfect, one accommodates my business cards, another my keys, which is a blessing for accessibility, and the zipper section plays host to my cell phone.

The bottom of the bag holds stick colognes, a small make-up bag, my laminated "I AM" affirmations, a couple of name badges, a broken step counter (lol), and a variety of pens.

Have you ever thought about how many shades of black exist? Literally, there could be close to fifty. What a wide variation! Chances are you may have heard that, "Variety is the spice of life." Well, that statement is just as true when it comes to black as dirt, there are many kinds and very expensive. According to Cornell University, the darker the soil, the higher the level of organic matter. Dirt is used for many purposes and one of its common usages is to grow things. Without it, trees, plants, grass, vegetation etc., possess no chance of growing naturally and neither can humans! Have you ever considered, "that it is in your dirt, where you have garnered great strength?" Dirt matters.

In life, we have a tendency, to bury our dirty little secrets. Sometimes in life, we have deep dark secrets, which we carefully attempt to hide in fear that someone might discover them. My grandmother was relentless for saying, "...some secrets, I will die with." I wonder how many of us have secrets which are killing us. Are your roots, choking your fertile ground?

Earlier I eluded to how much I enjoyed my black bag and noting I tend to use it allot.

I think this is a suitable place to permit my well-made, sleek, and chic little black purse to speak. Be quiet and listen intently, it is admonishing you to deal with your dirt.

Envision your perfect little black bag, emptying out your dirty secrets, where the top soil has been excavated from debris and rocks. The load will become lighter and can no longer weigh you down. Perhaps you were younger and made a gross error or just found yourself in a compromising position, but today, you have an opportunity to start another mound. Whatever amount of dirt you might have, regardless of how black and gritty, God will forgive you.

From time to time, we all need to try something different. While empirically you had some great successes, I challenge you to break the cycles of conformity and share your dirt with the right person, who will help and not hurt you. Redefining the status quo, could open up doors that you never knew existed. You have to be open to change. Allow me to encourage you to be as organic as you can be. Your life matters and you don't have to be held hostage by your past.

Power Red

Because I am a girly-girl who really likes color, my red leather bag accompanies me to many galas. My main concern is not that it matches my outfit but rather it makes a statement. Out of all my bags, I carry the least content in this one. Although it's lighter, it makes the greatest impact.

Basically, this purse carries my identification. Regardless of where I go, it is proof positive of my identity. No-one has the exact ID number as me. Without question no-one has the exact DNA as me and I am self-assured of who God made me to be. Whether walking into an event alone or being escorted by a knight in shining armor, my confidence is unshakable. If my ID read John Doe, I would be concerned, but I can vouch for myself; and so can you! Regardless of how people address you, only answer to the identity which God gave you. Remember, like my red bag, less is inside the bag, but know that less can be more. This bag boldly states that I am not trying to blend in, but to stand out.

Though I am a part of several teams and I endorse teamwork, I understand there are times when I must go it alone. Acceptance of self is key! When you agree with yourself, right where you are, you command presence. It is here, when the door of possibility swings wide open. Create your own fashion rules. Once you accept you, the change you make will be self-motivated. You will not be concerned with all the confinements of another person's success. Look in your purse, pull out your ID and commend yourself on your awesomeness!

Only change what you know needs changing. Don't lie to

yourself nor be defined by another person's rules. Today, start with the acceptance of all your shortcomings. Transform your belief system to transition into the new you. *You* lead and let others follow you!

Imagine looking at your ID saying, "This is me now". Then picture you later. What does that mental picture look like? Hopefully a profile of confidence and prosperity.

You are to stand out and not to blend in. Perfect, by definition, does not exist. You are you, uniquely. Be content but not complacent and be satisfied without settling. We are all a work in progress.

So, if you feel rejected, reaffirm yourself. No doubt, rejection is painful, but it is short-lived. You did nothing wrong, you decided to defy the norm and walk in your difference by sporting an empty red purse. It's possible someone else might not understand your fashion sense, but it's your **pursonality**. Whatever you do, don't get caught up in the deception of the opinion of others. They have been strategically sent to overthrow your conquering spirit. Lest I remind you, you are fearfully and wonderfully created by God.

So, tell me, *who's* opinion really matters? No more needs to be said. Search for meaning through serving others not acceptance. Don't be fooled by the mirage of money, status, promotion, popularity and celebrity. Incidentally, prominence is not important unless used to regard others.

Consent to your own reality. Be assured you have everything you need to achieve your goal. Accept others; don't berate yourself. Your value will shine through. You are okay, even before you arrive at your chosen destination.

Summing up the contents in my **_pursonality_** can only be described with one word, *intentional*. Intentions without desire manifest very little power. My desire is to live in the now. For me, that means being prepared and having the things I need ready when I need them. Intentions augment the law of attraction however, you must take the first step. My purse will always have a couple of nice pens, because throughout the day, I anticipate writing or taking notes. Therefore, I take the time to carefully choose what I place in my handbag.

I switch out my handbags regularly because they are a part of my attire. It's a reminder for all of us that change is not change unless we change. It's your future. Avenge your knowledge, seize your intellectual endowment, whether great or small, progress in your change. Remember, change is not contingent upon past deeds but on changing your present actions. This effort requires a small bit of planning.

Transferring my items from bag to bag also keeps me abreast of what I need to add, replace or remove. My tissue seems to get the worst end of the deal and is rarely used because it's crumpled, but the hand sanitizer has become my most trusted partner. Sanitizer is a sign of the times. *My sisters . . .* every time you clean your hands, let it be a reminder of staying pure before the Lord.

May the contents of your purse be symbolic of the contents of your heart!

Purse Prayer:

Dear God,

Anoint this sister reading this piece. Embrace her tightly and whisper in her ear that she was fashioned after Your likeness for her good and Your glory. Remind her that your promises are "yeah & amen." Encourage her to prophesy to her dry bones that they shall live and not die. Tell her that she has time because time is not a factor in You. Your Word says, "...be still and know that..." You are God. You are a God of seasons and this one has been anointed just for her.

Amen.

Dr. Cynthia Harper

Dr. Cynthia Harper is the founder of **C.Harper Enterprises** and **My Favorite Charities® (MFC)**, a national community development organization specializing in building healthy communities, healthy camaraderie and developing healthy competition. She is a graduate of the University of Phoenix with a BS/BM degree with a concentration in Business.

She has also received an honorary PhD by Circa University. A native of Texas, Cynthia has called Atlanta home for more than twenty five years.Cynthia is a dedicated advocate for women and is purposed to speak and enlist others to "Discover their Purpose" and she loves supporting and sharing the narrative of grass root non-profits.

Dr. Cynthia Harper is the recipient of several awards including the 2017-2018 Worldwide Delegate by International organization, Dress for Success for "demonstrating unparalleled leadership and civic responsibility," 2016; Lifetime Achievement Award, by the 44th President of the United States of America; and 2014 beneficiary of Millennium Award by national non-profit, Diamond In The Rough for "Outstanding Community Service."

Cynthia is an Author, Professional Speaker, Trainer, Program Developer, Facilitator and Radio Host. She is the producer of many projects which empowers others to fulfill their Purpose. She is very active in community intiatives serving multiple non-profits.

Chapter 14

More Than Just A Purse

As you can see through the purse stories shared in this book, a woman's purse is a lot more than a pretty adornment hanging from her wrist or shoulder. It's a lot more than a container for random items that may or may not serve a purpose in her day-to-day life. It's a lot more than the fringe, frills and fashion labels carefully stitched on its outer layer. A lot more, my friend. Our purses truly hold our sacred secrets, tell our stories, take the shape of our lives and embrace the consistent change that we experience through all life's twists and turns. They truly do talk.

The question is, who's listening?

I was saddened by the suicide death of well-known fashion designer, Kate Spade; a woman who knew a lot about the inside and outside of a woman's purse. It makes me wonder what hurtful truths or painful secrets were in the bottom of her purse that were too painful to share with anyone in her circle of friends and family. What damage was caused to the inner lining of her "purse" that she felt was beyond repair? I'm sure if her purse could talk it may have desperately alerted her friends and family to the dangers that lied ahead.

When I discussed the concept of this project with the contributing authors in this book, the one major point each of us felt strongly about was the importance of transparently sharing our stories to ensure no woman felt alone in her season of struggle. When we openly share our truth, we help one another take a deep breath and find the strength to persevere. You're not alone and you can rest easy knowing that we can relate.

But, now the time has come for us to snap, latch and zip our purses closed and courageously carry them into the next amazing season of our lives. I hope you took full advantage of rummaging through our purses and examining the deep contents of their inner linings. Perhaps you discovered something new about yourself during this journey or maybe you were jolted out of your haze and into your current reality.

Whatever the case may be, I hope that you were encouraged and inspired enough to do some digging through your own purse and thoughtfully expose the contents within.

As I mentioned when you started this journey, maybe it's time for you to get quiet and do some self-reflecting.

Here are some questions that may help you get started. Spend time thoughtfully discovering the answers to these questions and see where they take you. You might be surprised by all that you are carrying.

1. What weight are you carrying that's too heavy to tote into the next season of your life?

2. What junk do you need to get rid of that's taking up valuable real estate in the container of your heart?

3. What truths do you need to say out loud so it no longer has a place to hide in the compartments of your soul?

4. What residue from lies that you believed have attached itself to your inner lining that you now need to disbelieve?

5. What treasures have you tucked away that need to be brought to the light?

This might be your time to revisit some experiences or confront and expose issues you've been avoiding. Or maybe it's time for you to tell your story of trial to triumph and how you overcame adversity. Your story may just be the lifeline that someone needs to hear in order to press forward another day.

Let me help you begin writing your purse story. In the space below, I invite you to provide an honest answer to the question:

"If your purse could talk, what would it say?"

_____

_____

_____

_____

_____

_____

_____

_____

_____

_____

_____

_____

_____

_____

_____

_____

_____

_____

_____

_____

_____

_____

_____

_____

_____

_____

_____

_____

_____

_____

_____

_____

_____

_____

To share your purse story and to be
encouraged by others who have courageously
shared their stories, please visit:

www.HerPurseStories.com

Thank You

To each of the contributing authors – my sisters...my purse posse...my prayer warriors –I sincerely thank you for saying "yes" to this project and trusting me with your stories. I am forever grateful for your courage and your transparency. I pray that God will expand your territories and fill your purses with blessings that you won't have room enough to receive.

DeYonne Parker

To learn more about DeYonne and the contributing authors

Visit: www.IfHerPurseCouldTalk.com

Email: info@DeYonneParker.com

Call: (404) 477-GEMS (4367)

21038115R00113

Made in the USA
Columbia, SC
16 July 2018